IT'S NOT ABOUT POLITICS, IT'S ABOUT PROPHECY

DAVID E. SIRIANO

WESTBOW
PRESS®
A DIVISION OF THOMAS NELSON
& ZONDERVAN

WestBow Press books may be ordered through booksellers or by contacting:

WestBow Press
A Division of Thomas Nelson & Zondervan
1663 Liberty Drive
Bloomington, IN 47403
www.westbowpress.com
1 (866) 928-1240

ISBN: 978-1-9736-8728-3 (sc)
ISBN: 978-1-9736-8727-6 (e)

Print information available on the last page.

WestBow Press rev. date: 04/02/2020

Dedication

To my wonderful and precious wife of 57 years, Elsa May Larson Siriano who stood with me for the first 45 years of ministry as Pastors. Also, she has traveled with me for the past 11 years after retirement while speaking at many churches about the Second Coming of Christ and the End-times.

Before I would stand to speak to congregations about the prophetic aspect of ministry, she would take the opportunity to address them about the practical side of ministry.

Many thanks and much admiration to her for her help in spreading the gospel of Jesus Christ over these many years.

Special Thanks

Special thanks to Pamela Amendola. She and her husband Rick Amendola are the Pastors of New Life Christian Assembly of God Church in Haverhill, MA. After speaking in their church, she told me that if I wrote a book about my sermon "It's not about Politics, it's about Prophecy" she would buy it.

That inspired me to continue putting my thoughts together about that subject that I had been working on for the past year. Her request caused me to put it in book form. Thank you Pamela!

Contents

Introduction

The political state of America is in a critical crisis. The rest of the world is no different. America and the world are mimicking past countries and empires that have existed for a time and then were removed after various periods of success and failure.

In "It's not about politics, it's about prophecy," there can be seen the rabid condition that American politics have become. The dichotomy in our political system is deafening. It seems that we have been divided into two contradictory entities that are unrecoverable. The things that we are facing in America that other nations have faced are:

(1) Grave internal immorality that cannot be changed because the course of direction in the nation has been severely altered from its earlier convictions.
(2) Horrible economic conditions that weaken the nation, which usually has an impact the rest of the world.
(3) A warlike machine that overstretches the military and causes a lack of desire in that nation to fight in future wars.
(4) Cultural differences that are good for a time but then marginalizes the various people groups in the nation and fractures its unity, authority, and power.
(5) Polarization of the political powers between those who are in office and have the majority in any presiding political body,

and those who are in the minority and oppose the policies of the presiding majority.

This book speaks about the fact that the Bible is a prophetic book and that God has used America for His literal prophetic plan for Israel, the Church in the End Times. We are made to understand that God is the Supreme Authority in the world. There is no other God. He knows about things from the beginning of time until the end of time, and He is in control of all things pertaining to politics and the ensuing prophetic plans for the world.

Chapter One
God's Prophetic Plan

IT'S NOT ABOUT POLITICS

Politics can be good. It is involved with governing a country, state or a city and is meant to understand the needs of its citizens, and serve with them in mind. It makes decisions that affect finances, issues and ideas, and it governs with care for all.

The problem is that politics has a tendency to severely split a country into two or more political opinions and philosophies. There is nothing wrong with a two party political system if used in a correct manner, but politicians in America have created a strong disunity instead of a strong democracy. It has caused our politicians and people to have a deep lack of respect for each other. Our country has been split into factions and self-seeking judgments and views.

The Devil is in the mix of all the bad politics and sinful behavior around the world and not just in America. He is always trying to take control of this world away from God. Also, he is always trying to appeal to and influence the sinful nature of man. We read in the scripture about the sin in the last days and we know that the Devil is the instigator behind this behavior, even in politics.

> The Devil is in the mix of all the bad politics and sinful behavior in the world.

II Timothy 3:1-7 says. "In the last days there will be very difficult times. For people will love only themselves and their money. They will be boastful and proud, scoffing at God, disobedient to their parents, and ungrateful. They will consider nothing sacred. They will be unloving and unforgiving; they will slander others and have no self-control. They will be cruel and hate what is good. They will betray their friends, be reckless, be puffed up with pride, and love pleasure rather than God. They will act religious, but they will reject the power that could make them godly. Never able to understand the truth." (NLT)

It is so easy to look at all the confusing political climate that is engulfing America and the world that many of us fail to see the prophetic plan that God is using to bring the dramatic events of this worldliness to a godly conclusion. Some do not know or understand the basis of the scripture and how God can speak to us in a spiritual way.

Because the world looks so much at politics, we who are on the sidelines fail to seek the wisdom and will of God. We then take sides with one political power or position against another, rather than show the love of God.

It is best to live in love as it says in I John 4:7-8, "Love comes from God. Those who love are God's children and they know God. Those who do not love do not know God because God is love." (NLV)

Without the love of God the political world is at odds with each other. We find ourselves being a part of the divisive climate and polarization that is happening in our nation and the world. Many times we sacrifice friendship and harmony as we take sides against others. Sometimes we differ with those who are in the Christian faith and we lose our love and care in the body of Christ. It has become fierce and competitive. The world looks at things politically and of course never seems to understand or grasp what God is doing prophetically.

Without the love of God we live in an incomprehensible darkness that doesn't know what God is doing. It is a darkness that is just the opposite of any visible light. Without God's love we are at odds with those who differ with us or have a different opinion. This is when politics becomes drastic. We need to come out of the darkness and respond to the Word of God and practice a true love of God with others, and not evil. God's word says to live in the light.

> Isaiah 8:20 says, "Look to God's instructions and teachings! People who contradict his word are completely in the dark." (NLT)

> John 3:19 says, "And this is the condemnation, that the light has come into the world, and men loved darkness rather than light, because their deeds were evil." (NKJV)

Sometimes politicians and other leaders who are in the public consciousness speak words that only pertain to their political view. They avoid or come in conflict with the political views of others. Many times they take things out of context and emphasize what they see and never seem to understand or appreciate what others may see. We then join in the political fray and find ourselves angry and distraught with others, and with the world.

We can become so adamant about politics that we fail to respect someone else's political persuasion. Now, there is nothing wrong with viewing a political situation that may differ with those persuaded by another political understanding or political view. It is not wrong to see things in a different light than our neighbor or friend. It can be wrong if you make your view the "only" view or the "final answer" even if it means sacrificing friendship.

Many times we do not check the background or items that we are hearing about or viewing on television or the internet and we pass the information on to others. Most of the time we do not know how to compare what we are seeing or hearing with scripture to make sure that it agrees with God's Word before we pass it along.

We should conclude that the Bible indicates that God is in control of all things whether good or bad. He knows how to turn evil things into good for His honor and glory as He develops and brings about His prophetic plan. That's what makes Him a Sovereign God!

People may disagree on politics but should work together with love and compassion. We forget that the Bible is both liberal and conservative. It is conservative when it comes to holding to the obedience of God's laws and ways, and maintaining existing godly views or conditions of belief. It may also be more cautious toward others who are not willing to stand for righteously living the word of God.

Liberalism is not as strict in the observance of traditional or established forms or ways, and will many times be open minded to living without any restraint. It will also be liberal when it comes to helping others and lifting them up in their time of need.

So together, as far as the Bible is concerned, you need to hold to a conservative view, uphold God's law, and keep all things within the bounds of the law. Then you also need to have a liberal view and use the power of the law to do everything you can without breaking the law, but help others. As far as the Bible is concerned, it has both conservative and liberal views.

What is happening to America? It seems as if politics has gone crazy and that it is out of control. Politics is a force and it grips people's hearts. Is it true that no one is practicing restraint and that everyone is seeking to destroy others who do not believe like them?

Democrats have a different view or agenda than republicans and republicans have a different view or agenda than democrats. Criticism from both parties has become more divisive than ever before in recent memory. A cruel and hateful attitude can be seen in nearly all who participate in political conversations and debates. Their political congressional committees rankle with severe animosity. It seems as if our political system has been demonized and there is no solution in sight. Our politics have become polarized and it's worse than most of us have ever seen in our lifetime.

The only thing that seems to matter is if they win or their party wins. Much of it is seen and endorsed by the press and many times only half of the truth is reported, the half they want their viewers to see and hear. Sometimes the truth becomes stretched until it becomes a lie.

IT'S ABOUT PROPHECY

> Politics has a tendency to divide people, but prophecy has a tendency to unite people.

Politics has a tendency to divide people, but prophecy has a tendency to unite people. So when we see the political climate in America and around the world we must remember that God uses nations and leaders. Whether good or bad, it brings His prophetic plan to the forefront so that we can safely say that "It's not about politics, it's about prophecy."

When we're talking about prophecy, we're not talking about personal prophecy to individuals, although that may have its place. Prophecy as our subject is referring to, is speaking and teaching about a future time when the evil conditions of the world come to a climax. God enters the world stage by sending His Son Jesus Christ to earth a second time with the Church, to rule and reign for a thousand years before He makes a New Heaven and a New Earth.

So how and where do we find out what God is doing without believing all of the tantalizing sensationalistic hype that we hear in the news or see on the social networks? We find the answer in God's Word. In order to find out what God is doing in the future, we have to find out what He's done in the past. We have to keep His word in the forefront of our minds at all times.

The question is not, "how should I try to understand all of the views of politics, or how do I combat the political views that I disagree with?" Rather, the question should be "what does God see, and how does He control the nations and leaders of the world to bring about His prophetic biblical plan?" How can we be a part of that?

> In Jeremiah 1:10, God told that prophet, "See, I have this day set thee over the nations and over the kingdoms, to root out, and to pull down, and to destroy, and to throw down, to build, and to plant." (KJV)

Try to understand what God is doing to the nations. Pray just like we would pray for a personal answer to prayer. As we pray for God to move things and change things in our own lives for His will to be done, we should pray in the same manner for God's will to be done in the nations. This should cause us to always keep in mind that "It's about Prophecy."

The prophetic landscape in God's Word should cause our prayer to be, "Lord, help me to understand how you are shaping the events of the nations of the world so that people will believe in you and your plans for a future kingdom in Heaven."

The many problems in our world seem to escape those who do not care or understand that God has a master biblical plan for the end of the world as we know it. We have politicians and even some religious leaders who do not get the fact that God uses the politics of leaders and nations to arrive at His own prophetic conclusions. We have to trust God and believe that He knows what He's doing.

At times, Christians have the tendency to ignore the line by line interlocking statements given by God in scripture but accept the out of balance theories that tickle the imagination. They take the biblical ideas that sound good and that appear to be given by God, yet they don't know how to fit them into any sound eschatological (end times) interpretation or overall plan.

They do not know how to use the scriptures to balance out their view so that it can bring logical and common sense conclusions. Scripture encourages us to learn how to balance our thoughts by carefully using God's Word.

> I Corinthians 2:13-14 says, "These things we also speak, not in words which man's wisdom teaches but which the Holy Spirit teaches, <u>comparing spiritual things with spiritual.</u> But the natural man does not receive the things of the Spirit of God, for they are foolishness to him; nor can he know *them,* because they are spiritually discerned." (NKJV)

So how do we compare "spiritual things with spiritual?" Anyone with a remedial understanding of the book of Revelation or Daniel can talk about the Tribulation, the Antichrist or the Millennium. That part is easy. What must be done is for us to take one scripture, read it in light of another supportive interlocking scripture, and compare the one spiritual thought with the other spiritual thought. Our conclusion must be a proper balance of scripture without the danger of a private, dangerous and sensationalist out of balance interpretation of scripture.

> In II Peter 1:19-21 it warns us with these words, "And so we have the prophetic word confirmed, which you do well to heed as <u>a light that shines in a dark place, until the day dawns and the morning star rises in your hearts</u>; knowing this first, that <u>no prophecy of Scripture is of any private interpretation, for prophecy never came by the will of man</u>, but holy men of God spoke *as they were* moved by the Holy Spirit." (NKJV)

The word 'private' in that scripture means a word of prophecy that comes from one's self or it is their own message, and therefore belongs to them. It means that God did not give it to them but they conjured it up within themselves.

The word 'interpretation' means the unloosing of a message in order to decide, settle, or explain something that is hard to understand. If it is an interpretation not balanced with scripture, it may lead you down the wrong path. The scary thing is what the Bible says about those kind of prophets. In Jeremiah 14:14 and 23:16 it says this:

> And the LORD said to me, "The prophets prophesy lies in my name. I have not sent them, commanded them, nor spoken to them; they prophesy to you a false vision, divination, a worthless thing, and the deceit of their heart." (NKJV)

8

Thus says the LORD of hosts: "Do not listen to the words of the prophets who prophesy to you. They make you worthless; they speak a vision of their own heart, not from the mouth of the LORD." (NKJV)

We have to be careful about the prophecy we may hear and hold on to, or the prophecy we may hear and pass on to someone else. We must have the confidence that any message we hear is truly from God.

What we have to see is God's step by step planned message from Him that fits the entire Bible from the book of Genesis to the book of Revelation. A prophetic unified light shines throughout the entire Bible. As it says in the scripture, there is, "a light that shines in a dark place, until the day dawns and the morning star rises in your hearts." (II Peter 1:19 KJV) That is a beautiful picture of Christ as He fulfills prophecy.

To help us understand about God and what He is saying through His prophetic word, we also need the power of the Holy Spirit working in our lives. His word can be poured out so that we can speak about the End Times in a prophetic manner. In this 21st century, He can use us whether we are young or old. He can use our children, and our co-workers. This is what God says about how He does that in the last days:

Acts 21:17-18 says, 'And it shall come to pass in the last days, says God, that I will pour out my Spirit on all flesh; your sons and your daughters shall prophesy, your young men shall see visions, your old men shall dream dreams. And on my menservants and on my maidservants I will pour out my Spirit in those days and they shall prophesy." (PHILLIPS)

God's plan ends with His will being done in the world and in our lives. What also helps us to understand prophecy, is that all prophecy must be viewed to have literally happened in the past, or will literally happen in the future. It should only be interpreted symbolically when it cannot be interpreted in a literal way. And even then, you have to do that very carefully.

Nothing involving God's plan of salvation and His emphasis on His purpose deviates from this pattern. In the Old Testament, God's plan involved the Nation of Israel and in the New Testament it is involving the Church of Jesus Christ. Both the Nation of Israel and the Church bring God's prophetic plan to a conclusion and opens the door to God's creation of a New Heaven and a New Earth.

After the current Heaven and Earth pass away, the New Jerusalem, which is described in the Book of Revelation as the Bride of Christ, will be situated in the New Heaven and Earth that God will create. It will be created with an emphasis and inclusion of both the Nation of Israel and the Church. It has twelve gates with the names of the Twelve Tribes of Israel written on them and it has twelve foundations with the names of the Twelve Apostles written on them.

Both the Nation of Israel and the Church are inscribed in the future world to come. This is God's plan and will for the future of the world today, and it will lead us into the future of the world for tomorrow.

We have to understand the benefit of the word of God as it relates to Bible prophecy. It will lead us out of a political quagmire that many of us are in, and into the freedom of understanding God's prophetic plans that He has for the future.

PROPHECY AND POLITICS

How do we understand both "prophecy and politics" without confusion? It's simple. We know that "religion (belief, faith) and politics (governments)" are the only two systems that are found in the Bible. "Religion and politics" or according to our subject "prophecy and politics," came in the form of Patriarch's and Prophets, Judges and Kings.

All other functions that may even be in a network of related kingdoms, organizations, institutions or groups of people, come under the umbrella of "religion and politics." You cannot talk about religion without talking about politics and you cannot talk about politics without talking about religion. All other systems are part of or are influenced by religion and politics throughout the entire Bible.

There has always been Prophets and Kings in the Bible. Many times the two have been in conflict with each other. God allowed politics, but it has always been under His prophetic persuasion or control. The prophets of God spoke prophetically to the nations, its leaders and people about the things that God wanted, what He was doing, and what He wanted to do. Prophecy played an important role in the politics of the nations. All of God's plans had, and continue to have a prophetic conclusion.

> If you want to understand "prophecy and politics" you have to understand politics in light of Bible prophecy.

If you want to understand "prophecy and politics" you have to understand politics in light of Bible prophecy. Also, if you want to understand what God is doing with America and what He is doing with the other nations of the world, again, you have to understand politics in light of Bible prophecy. Prophecy is a major part of religion and God acts on politics to accomplish His prophetic will.

When interpreted correctly, religion is or should be very prophetic. It speaks about the things of the past and of the future. It reveals the heart of God and what He wants for the people who are obedient to Him. It also reveals the destruction of those who do not follow Him. The prophets either spoke to 'forth-tell' the news about God to the people of their day, or they spoke to 'foretell' the news of the events that were going to happen in the future.

Today, the struggle between right and wrong in the prophetic state of America and other nations of the world is at a critical state. God can either bless the nations, including America, or He can destroy them. It all depends on that nation's willingness to turn from just political views, so that they can obey God and His commands that are very clear in the Bible.

> Jeremiah 18:7-10 gives this prophetic word about the nations, "The instant I speak concerning a nation and concerning a kingdom, to pluck up, to pull down, and to destroy it, if that nation against whom I have spoken turns from its evil, I will relent of the disaster that I thought to bring upon it. And the instant I speak concerning a nation and concerning a kingdom, to build and to plant it, if it does evil in my sight so that it does not obey my voice, then I will relent concerning the good with which I said I would benefit it." (NKJV)

If God is planning to destroy a nation because of its evil ways, but that nation repents, God will forgive them and not destroy it. If God builds up a nation and they turn away from God and commit evil and not obey Him, God will not bless them. In order to avoid disaster for America, we need to believe that America can have spiritual revival, despite what is happening in politics.

GOD SPOKE THROUGH PROPHETS

The great prophet Jeremiah mentioned how much speaking the word of God meant to him.

> We find this powerful scripture in Jeremiah 20:8: "But if I say, "I will not remember Him or speak any more in His name," then in my heart it is like a burning fire shut up in my bones. I am tired of holding it in, and I cannot do that." (NLV)

At first, Jeremiah didn't want to speak, but he couldn't hold back. As the scriptures reveal, God plays an integral part in the nations of the world. Prophets like Jeremiah have always been a voice for God to the nations in both the Old Testament and the New Testament.

The prophets knew of God's unfolding plans for Israel by understanding and speaking about these three critical areas of past, present and future:

1. **The History** of what God did for them in the past so that they could learn to change the future. All of the prophets seemed to know their history.
2. **The Current state of politics** and how God would deal with nations. The prophets spoke to the current events of their time and their connection and interplay between the nations. Today we call that political science.
3. **The Prophetic** things that God would reveal to them so that they could tell what would happen in the future, knowing that history repeats itself. That future understanding is called "Eschatology."

Even today, by using these same three methods, it can be revealed to you what God is going to do in the future. You can see His plans unfolding to reach His prophetic goals.

God spoke these words to the Children of Israel through Moses and Amos on how He reveals His plans so that they could walk in obedience:

> Deuteronomy 29:29 says, "The secret things belong to the LORD our God, but those things which are revealed belong to us and to our children forever, that *we* may do all the words of this law." (NKJV)

> Amos 3:7 says, "Surely the Lord GOD does nothing, unless He reveals His secret to His servants the prophets." (NKJV)

God who knows all things is the one who raises up the nations and destroys them. He allows them to rise and then collapse so that their dominance is only for a certain period of time. He raises up the leaders of those nations and He removes them for His purpose and plans. That's how He controls the nations. That is how He uses and controls politics in order to bring about His will for prophecy.

He uses the power and understanding of prophecy that influences everything, and puts everything under His control. This includes determining the boundaries and the times of the existence of nations, and its leaders. The following scriptures explain exactly how God does it:

> "And He has made from one blood every nation of men to dwell on all the face of the earth, and has determined their <u>pre-appointed times</u> and the <u>boundaries of their dwellings</u>." Acts 17:26 (NKJV)

> "For the kingdom is the LORD'S and He rules over the nations." Psalm 22:28 (NKJV)

"He delivers up nations before him and subdues kings. He makes them like dust with his sword, as the wind-driven chaff with his bow." Isaiah 41:2 (NASB)

In the Bible, prophets spoke to kings, and they have spoken to many leaders since that time. If we are going to talk about America and the prophetic state it is in, we have to rely on the Bible as our source of understanding. Just as there have been prophets to the kingdoms in the Bible, there have been prophets to America as well. There have been prophets to America in the past, there are many prophets who are speaking to America today in their locality or region, and there will be prophets to America in the future.

However, it is safe to say that Billy Graham who died in 2018, is probably the last great prophet to America before changes come, and before the coming of the Lord. No prophet has spoken to as many American Presidents as Evangelist Billy Graham has. Out of the forty-five Presidents of America, he met with thirteen of them, from Harry Truman to Donald Trump, speaking to Trump prior to his becoming President.

Since the end of WW II when America helped Israel to be established in her land once again as the focus of the world, the Presidents saw Graham's life as a Christian light for God's plan for the world before the return of Christ! He was there to witness to and pray for the Presidents during various critical times in American history. No other clergyman was ever in that position for that long of a time. He was God's Pastor to the Presidents!

The timing of his ministry was key to America! After Billy Graham, who will witness to our leaders in the waning years of America as a great superpower? Who will speak to our leaders just like the great prophets in the days of the Bible! Pray for America!

THE PROPHETIC PLAN

In a line by line interpretation and understanding of the Word of God, His prophetic plan included first a couple, then a family, then a nation of people, and finally a Church that is now scattered around the entire world winning and helping those who are far from God.

All of this plan is because God first of all loved His creation when He planted that love in Adam and Eve, the first man and woman. He then shared that love with a particular man called Abraham who walked perfect before Him. That man started a family whose family then became a nation.

This love broadened to include other nations and masses of people around the world that would find that love and follow a God that would sacrifice His own nature for a creation of people that had fallen into disobedience and sin.

The world had lost its way and had to re-discover and know the God of creation and love. His plan was a step by step progression that was interconnected, and which seems to rise as if one is climbing or ascending a path or mountain.

> Through Jesus Christ, God put Himself into the world that He created, to understand it, to show how to deal with sin, and overcome it.

Through Jesus Christ, God put Himself into the world that He created, to understand it, to show how to deal with sin, and overcome it. His perfect nature was satisfied with the payment for that sin when He put Himself in the place of sinful people and died for them through the death of His Son Jesus Christ on the cross of Calvary. He satisfied His anger by dealing with sin and giving Himself in our place in this manner. Our only hope was for God to rescue us. He was the only one as a perfect sacrifice that could have done it or else He would have had to wipe out His entire creation.

Other people and nations of the world that God allowed to come to power, found themselves at odds with the family of Abraham and also with the one nation that God had formed for His prophetic purpose.

Nevertheless, this was God's way to bring about a pathway of deliverance from sin for a chosen nation and finally for a chosen body of believers, the Church. The Church of course owes its love, strength and foundation to Jesus Christ. It also owes its basis of understanding of who God is to the Nation of Israel because of the earlier teachings given to them by God.

In our day and time, after all of the scriptures were written and the Church age had brought Christianity to the world, what was God going to do prophetically in the future and how was He going to do it? After all of the mighty nations in the Bible and throughout the centuries that God worked with since then, what was the next powerful nation that would be His prophetic voice and plan for the End Times?

In trying to understand all of this, it is ludicrous to squabble over politics, because politics cannot hold a candle to prophecy. We have to always remember this key phrase:

"IT'S NOT ABOUT POLITICS, IT'S ABOUT PROPHECY"

Chapter Two
America's Turn

WHAT WAS GOD GOING TO DO?

After the death of Christ, the Nation of Israel that God promised to Abraham as an everlasting covenant was destroyed and no longer a nation. It existed no more. The questions that history should ask is, "was God going to bring Israel back to life?" If He was, "how was He going to do it?" "Who would He use in order to further His plan for prophecy?" "What nation would rise to power to help resurrect the nation that was to be no more?"

God had to use the politics of the world to unveil His Sovereign prophetic will. As history proved, God was going to put into action one of the most recent superpowers in existence for the end times, the United States of America. America is not mentioned in the Bible but it is easy to compare it to nations that are. Biblical nations rose to power and greatness, had a tendency to fail God, then they would finally fall from God's mercy and grace because of their sin and disobedience. America is no different.

> America is not mentioned in the Bible but it is easy to compare it to nations that are.

What is happening in America and the world must be understood in God's prophetic biblical design. First of all, God's relationship with the world must be seen through His continual Covenant relationship with the Nation of Israel in the Old Testament. Anything outside of that, will totally miss what God is doing in the world today and what He will do in the future. <u>Second</u>, everything is about Israel, it is centered in prophecy, and God has used the Church in the New Testament and beyond to point to the Second Coming of Jesus Christ.

The scriptures show that besides the Jewish people being restored 500 years before the time of Christ after their captivity in Babylon, God was going to restore Israel a second time before Jesus Christ returns. That second time happened in 1948 and God used America to do so. The return of Israel is one of the great reasons for the birth of America.

All this happened and is now influencing God's Prophetic Worldwide plan for the End Times which includes a massive time of tribulation for the world, and a Millennium in which Christ will reign in a time of rest for the world.

GOD USED AMERICA

Within 150 years after the end of the Revolutionary War (1775-1783), the British Empire was beginning to collapse. God needed America as another political superpower other than Britain so that His plans for the Middle East could continue to be unveiled in the future. God needed America to help reestablish the nation of Israel in Palestine for the 20th and 21st Centuries.

The Ottoman (Islam) Empire fought against the Jews over the centuries, the British Empire helped the Jews at first but then turned against them. Both of those empires collapsed. So now it was America's turn.

America has stood with Israel because God had a plan to establish them as a nation for the last days. America has been blessed of God because it put Him first at its early development, even before it started of a nation. It has also been blessed by God because of its extraordinary support of the right for Israel to exist.

> Psalm 33:10-12 says "The Lord brings the counsel of the nations to nothing; He makes the plans of the peoples of no effect. The counsel of the Lord stands forever, the plans of His heart to all generations. <u>Blessed *is* the nation whose God *is* the Lord</u>, the people He has chosen as His own inheritance." (NKJV)

> In Genesis 12:2-3 God told Abraham, "I will make you a great nation; I will bless you and make your name great; and you shall be a blessing. <u>I will bless those who bless you</u>, and I will curse him who curses you; and in you all the families of the earth shall be blessed." (NKJV)

Even though Israel willfully sinned, was disobedient, and had been severely disciplined by God, they still remained God's people and timepiece of prophecy. That's the way it began in the book of Genesis when God established the Nation of Israel and that's the way it will end in the book of Revelation. As chosen by God, they have been restored in their land for a prophetic purpose, and that purpose is the return of Jesus Christ.

In actuality, Israel has a special relationship with God like no other nation. In a sense it is a microcosm of the relationship that God longs for with the rest of the world. His love for the world is seen in the scriptures.

John 3:16. It says, "For God so loved the world that He gave His only begotten Son, that whosoever believeth in Him should not perish, but have everlasting life." (KJV)

PRESIDENTS AND THE MIDDLE EAST

God has used leaders of superpowers in the past and He has used the Presidents of America for today as well. They are important whether you like them or not and whether or not you agree with their politics or behavior. In the Bible, not all of the Kings of Israel and Judah were acceptable Kings. In fact, after Saul, David and Solomon, of the approximately 40 Kings that came after them, 30 of them are considered evil or wicked Kings.

Therefore, it is very important to pray for our leaders, pray for the Middle East and "pray for the peace of Jerusalem." God has prepared that part of the world for events that will happen in the future. Events that are a prelude and set-up for the peace signings in the future that will involve the Antichrist during the Great Tribulation.

When we think about events like that, the importance of the American Presidency cannot be overemphasized. Like the leaders of the biblical nations and other nations since that time, we must try to understand all of the American Presidents who may have had an influence on prophecy as God guides the nations.

If we want to understand Bible prophecy, we should not look at what the Presidents do that we don't like. If we focus strongly on what we may deem to be bad, we may never understand how God is using their policies, both good and bad as part of His master prophetic plan. We should try to find out what their decisions and policies are doing to advance God's will.

To understand the administration of any current President or the administration of any past President for that matter, you have to seriously consider that God is the one who puts leaders in power whether for good or evil, and you have to believe that He also removes them.

> God is the one who puts leaders in power whether for good or evil, and you have to believe that He also removes them.

Daniel 2:21 says that God "changes the times and the seasons; He removes kings and raises up kings; He gives wisdom to the wise and knowledge to those who have understanding." (NKJV)

Notice that it takes wisdom and knowledge to understand this! The understanding is that God not only controls the existence and removal of Kings but He is in charge of the times and the duration of things. He even directs the heart of the king in seasons or sets of appointed times.

Also, Psalm 75:6-7 says, "For exaltation *comes* neither from the east nor from the west nor from the south. But God *is* the Judge: He puts down one, and exalts another." (NKJV)

Proverbs 21:1 says, "In the LORD's hand the king's heart is a stream of water that he channels toward all who please him." (NIV)

God has marvelously used the Presidents and their policies that affect the Middle East for the End Times. We must therefore do what the Bible instructs us to do and that is to respect the leader of the people. We are also told to pray for them. God's word makes it clear.

Acts 23:5 says, "You must not speak evil of any of your rulers." (NLT)

I Timothy 2:1-3 says, "I urge you, first of all, to pray for all people. Ask God to help them; intercede on their behalf, and give thanks for them. Pray this way for kings and all who are in authority so that we can live peaceful and quiet lives marked by godliness and dignity. This is good and pleases God our Savior." (NLT)

Today, as we read about the Middle East, we realize that it has taken centuries to prepare the world for such a time as this. Prophetically speaking, we can see the part of God's plan which includes the lessening of the global power of America as a superpower around the world.

This is happening so that a shift of power can now move to the nations north and east of Israel in order for those nations to rise stronger in the future. These powers will rise to come against the nation of Israel in the last days.

God has used America's leaders in the forming of these dramatic shifts. America will be involved in the last day's scenario but will not be quite the global power as it has been in the past. The Presidency has been a great part of these last day plans. The following 20th and 21st Century Presidents are grouped on how they have helped move the world closer to the Second Coming of Jesus Christ. They have been involved with numerous preludes of what the Book of Revelation shows of God's Covenant relationship with Israel being restored in the last days.

These modern day Presidents are not addressed here as to whether they were good or bad Presidents. They are listed and categorized because of their policies that made progressive changes that affected Israel, the various agreements to benefit Israel in Palestine, and the Confrontation of the armies from the north and east that will invade Israel in the future.

RECENT PRESIDENTS AND PROPHECY

1. **Major Changes to Israel** – Franklin Delano Roosevelt, Harry Truman, and Donald Trump.
    *   Roosevelt helped lead the way in the WW II conflict when Jews were being slaughtered by Adolf Hitler. After that war, the Jewish people established the nation of Israel as a sign in the last days and to prepare that land for the Second Coming of Christ. That war helped fulfill Prophecy that brought the Jews back to Palestine.
    *   America's recognition of Israel came with the Truman Presidency in 1948 after they declared statehood. The President immediately gave his support which influenced other world leaders to do the same. Israel had their land again as promised by God.
    *   Jerusalem was recognized as the capital of Israel by Trump in 2017. In the future, that will allow the cooperation among the various religious and political factions in that land. After that, the Antichrist will appear and Israel will be persecuted by the Devil and its enemies.
    *   Also, Trump made political and economic changes in America's relationship with Europe, Russia, and North Korea. These nations will now look to nations other than America for stability. This brought the focus back to Europe and Asia for the answers they will need in establishing Globalism. It prepares the way for the Antichrist who will rule globally, possibly from Europe or the Middle East.

2. **Israel Accords** – <u>Jimmy Carter</u> and <u>Bill Clinton</u>.
   - The 1978 Camp David accords under Carter were agreements for peace signed between Israel and Egypt.
   - The 1994 Oslo accords under Clinton were agreements for peace signed between Israel and the PLO. Both of these events are a prelude and sign of a future time when agreements of false peace and safety will be made with these nations when the Antichrist comes during the Great Tribulation.

3. **Confrontational Persuasion** (involving potential Armies of the North) – <u>John F. Kennedy</u>, <u>Lyndon Johnson</u>, <u>Ronald Reagan</u> and <u>Barack Obama</u>.
   - Confrontation with the USSR by Kennedy in the Cuban Missile Crisis of 1962 forced the USSR to pull their missiles out of Cuba. Because of that, their military influence will be centered and involved in the Middle East rather than in the Western Hemisphere. This refocus needed to take place before the coming of the Lord.
   - The controversial Vietnam War involved Johnson, as America supported South Vietnam while China and the Soviet Union supported North Vietnam. The war helped contribute to the eventual collapse of the Soviet Union before the End Times. In the future they will work with European nations for the invasion of Israel.
   - Political confrontation by Reagan also contributed to the collapse of the Soviet Union. That released their stranglehold on Eastern Europe. Europe will now be a great power as well in the last days in the invasion from the north into Israel.
   - Confrontation with the USSR (Russia) was made by Obama in 2014 when Russia took control of the Ukraine and Crimea. Armies of the north from Europe can now

come to invade Israel in the End Times via the Crimean Peninsula. Obama and the G-8 industrialized nations of France, Germany, Italy, England, Japan, America and Canada dismissed Russia from this economic group because of its action against the Ukraine.

4. **Middle East and Far East** (involving potential Armies of the East) – <u>Harry Truman</u>, <u>Richard Nixon</u>, <u>George Herbert Walker Bush</u>, and <u>George Walker Bush</u>.
   - Truman's role in the Korean Conflict helped stop Communism from advancing from the East further into South Korea and beyond. Those armies were halted for the time being because their march from the East toward Israel will come later at the Battle of Armageddon.
   - The other three Presidents dealt with Middle East nations such as Israel and Iraq, and also with the Far East nation of China. Asian nations on the world stage will eventually come together to prepare themselves for an invasion from the Far East into Israel and the Middle East at the Battle of Armageddon.

5. **Caretaker Presidents** – <u>Dwight Eisenhower</u> and <u>Gerald Ford</u>.
   - They kept America running smooth or helped spare it during or after difficult times. They were President during times of peace or settlement showing God's love and mercy in the midst of, or after change to America, or to the rest of the world.

JERUSALEM – THE CITY OF GOD

An American President declared Jerusalem the capital of Israel and moved its Embassy there. So what's all the fuss and fight about? It was done to further establish Israel's legitimate acceptance in the world. So why are the major religions of the world so entranced with that land? It's because the land of Israel and the city of Jerusalem belong to God and the major religions have an interest in it! They all want to worship God in the place of one of the most holy sites in the world. They have an attraction toward God and want to claim Jerusalem.

Prophetically speaking, God called the land of Israel His land, and God said He chose the city of Jerusalem for Himself. It is His land and His city despite all of the claims of the religions that are fighting over it. The scripture is clear on this.

> Prophetically speaking, God called the land of Israel His land, and God said He chose the city of Jerusalem for Himself.

In Joel 3:2, God says this about Israel, calling it His land: "I will also gather all nations, and will bring them down into the valley of Jehoshaphat, and will plead with them there for <u>my people and *for* my heritage Israel</u>, whom they have scattered among the nations, and <u>parted my land</u>" (KJV)

God has declared that the city of Jerusalem belongs to Him. He said in I Kings 11:36 that He wanted it to be His city so "...that my servant David may always have a <u>lamp</u> before Me in Jerusalem, <u>the city which I have chosen for myself, to put my name there</u>" (NKJV). See also: I Kings 14:21 (NKJV); II Chronicles 12:13 NKJV

Notice that God wanted a lamp before Him in Jerusalem for the sake of David His servant. Some may say that the lamp refers to the Church and that all of biblical prophecy is about the Church. However, the Church is bigger than a lamp. Christ referred to believers as "a city that is set on a hill cannot be hid." (Matthew 5:14 KJV) The Church has not been hidden for centuries as Israel was. The lamp represents the nation of Israel, partially hidden and nearly extinguished for nearly 1900 years until the Jewish people became a nation again.

Because it is His city, God decided in the book of Genesis to give Jerusalem and the land of Canaan (modern day Palestine) to Abraham's seed which was passed down through his son Isaac and grandson Jacob. It was not given to Abraham's son Ishmael who was birthed through Hagar, his wife's servant. It was given to Isaac.

Ishmael and his descendants were given other land which became the Arab countries headed up by twelve princes that presided over twelve countries (Genesis 25:16 KJV). Isaac, Ishmael and their children have been at odds with each other for over 4,000 years and that conflict will have to be resolved during the Great Tribulation.

> About Ishmael it says in Genesis 16:12, "And he will be a wild man; his hand will be against every man, and every man's hand against him…" (KJV)

In past conflicts, the city of Jerusalem and the land of Israel had been taken by the Arab people (Ishmael's seed) through conquest. After WW I and WW II, the city and land was then taken away from the Arabs and given back to the Jews as a sign to the world in the last days.

Then, through God's Prophetic plan on December 6, 2017, the 45th President of the United States Donald Trump, declared Jerusalem the capital of Israel. On May 14, 2018 he authorized the United States Embassy to be moved to Jerusalem to coincide with the 70th Anniversary of Israel's proclamation of independence in 1948.

Jerusalem and the land of Israel will play a key role during the Great Tribulation and the Battle of Armageddon.

Does all this mean anything? To many people the answer is NO! But to the overall prophetic landscape, the answer is a resounding YES! The plan has been developed and was put in place by God centuries ago. All of the confusion and warfare happening in the world today is just further steps to bring about the climax of the Church age, the Rapture of the Church, the Tribulation, the Second Coming of Christ, and the Millennium.

AMERICA AND END-TIMES BIBLE PROPHECY

God has had a covenant with the Nation of Israel since the book of Genesis and He uses superpowers in His fight against the Devil while using Israel as a sign of judgment to come. Because of Israel's sin and disobedience, God used many nations to punish His chosen people. God's vengeance soon fell on those nations who punished Israel because of their own sin and evil. Those nations who made war and took control of Israel at various times in the Bible were Egypt, Assyria, Babylon, Medo-Persia, Greece, and Rome. After Bible times, Israel again lost control of their land, and the Ottoman Empire (Arab/Islam) occupied Palestine for hundreds of years until the early 20th Century.

After America was victorious in WW I, the Jews were allowed to return to Palestine in great numbers. In WW II, President Franklin Delano Roosevelt and Premier Joseph Stalin from the USSR defeated Adolf Hitler who had killed millions of Jews. God used both Roosevelt and Stalin to defeat Hitler even though Stalin had killed just as many people as Hitler did.

The United States of America had to rise to superpower status in order for Israel to declare statehood. America fought those two world wars to help bring Israel back to the land of Palestine and helped set the stage before the End Times and before the coming of the Lord. At the end of WW II, the United Nations divided Palestine to allow the Jews to have permanent residence there with the Arabs.

An estimated total of 60-80 Million lives were lost in WW I and WW II. More than half of that number in those wars were the deaths of innocent civilians. There were numerous causes and reasons for those wars, but a prophetic reason stands out from among the rest. That reason was so that the Jews could return to their original land of Palestine a second time as a sign of the coming of the Lord and a fulfillment of the promise made by God.

The Jews did lose their land and temple after the time of Christ but returned to Palestine after WW I, and WW II. The loss of their land was the price that the Nation of Israel had to pay for their part in the crucifixion of Christ.

Some might say that God would have nothing to do with war and that God would not use war to accomplish His purposes. Actually, He did it time and time again in the Bible. War is the wrath of man and the instigation of the Devil, but the Bible says that God uses the wrath of man for His purpose.

> War is the wrath of man and the instigation of the Devil, but the Bible says that God uses the wrath of man for His purpose.

In fact, the Bible declares that God controls man's wrath. God wears the wrath of man like clothing and that by doing so, He will be ready for battle. He also reveals His anger.

> Psalm 76:10 says, "For the wrath of man shall praise you; with a remnant of wrath you will clothe *and* arm yourself." (AMP)

Romans 1:18 says, "But God shows his anger from heaven against all sinful, wicked people who suppress the truth by their wickedness." (NLT)

A NATION'S RISE AND FALL

When it comes to the End Times, we must not look at things politically, but prophetically. We cannot do it any other way. How do the superpowers and the leaders of these superpowers fit in with God's plan? What do they contribute toward God's overall plan even if it's in the smallest prophetic way?

Many of the leaders of superpowers have powerfully affected the world as they have led their nation to do good things, and many times they have led their nation to the brink of disaster. History is full of powers that have ruined the lives and countries of the nations they have made war against.

All dominating superpowers rise and eventually collapse, whether literally or culturally, including America. Some past powers have simply been de facto superpowers, but the influence of a superpower many times is over a vast majority of the earth's population and usually affects most of the entire world.

Because God is in control of all nations and their leaders, He always uses superpowers to govern the affairs of the world. Then their superpower status wanes. When God is finished with a superpower He discards them. He throws them on the "superpower trash heap of history." That's what God has done in the past and that's what He does today, and that is what He will do in the future.

The same holds true in America as we will see. Many things are contributing to America's collapse, including our current use of the law of impeachment of a President. In recent years, impeachment has turned into an ugly, untenable and polarized article in the U.S. Constitution.

In the first 185 years of America we have had only one impeachment, from 1789 when George Washington served as President until 1974 when Richard Nixon resigned as President. Since that time we have had two impeachments, and Nixon's could have been one as well because his tenure as President was on the way toward impeachment. That's two and almost a third impeachment in just the past 45 years. Again, almost three in only the past 45 years! That rapidity of impeachment doesn't bode well with the survival of a nation like America and neither will its current political system survive. How many Presidents in the future will be subject to political rancor and impeachment?

I'm not worried about the presidents who are impeached. They can take care of themselves. They will survive one way or another. I'm more concerned about America whose politics have been polarized. I'm concerned about our nation. It's on the verge of collapse.

America's rise and fall follows the course of past superpowers. Any superpower's influence over other nations of the world is in God's control, and at His direction and for His purpose. Nations rise and fall in at least one or more of these five ways:

1. **Militarily** – A great super-military power can have troops anywhere in the world and it usually wins its wars. It is involved in other nations to create influence that can either benefit or harm other nations.
2. **Global Policeman** – Superpower armies can be in any part of the world to stabilize any world problem and like a policeman, enforce its idea of peace.

3. **Politically** – Superpowers usually have international relationships with all of the major nations and even smaller nations as well.

4. **Economically** – Superpowers can influence the money markets of the world with their currency or their investments. Their currency many times is used in financial trade agreements.

5. **Culturally** – A superpower affects the world's morality, religion, language, art, science and technology as its influence is carried around the world. They can also help with the infrastructure of other countries. People from around the world come to the country of the superpower as they travel great distances to try and become a part of its culture.

GOD IS IN CONTROL

The Bible is very clear about God's influence in the affairs of the world. His power is still a key element as it guides each of the superpower nations to bring about His final solution to the world's problems. The Devil is still a major player in all of the confusion and power struggles of this world, but God has the final say. The following scriptures describes God's involvement with the nations.

> Job 12:23 says, "He makes nations great, and destroys them; He enlarges nations, and guides them." (NKJV)

> Isaiah 45:7 says, "...I send good times and bad times. I, the Lord, am the one who does these things." (NLT)

God is in control of the nations and He is in control of America. Some have said that 'America did not start as a godly nation.' They blame America for being evil because of its war, cruelty, dominance and burdens that were inflicted on others. True. That cannot be denied, but God is still in control of the nations for His will to be done. We have to remember that God uses both good people and bad people, good things and bad things, and good nations and bad nations.

Name one nation today that has ever started with godliness and yet did not have any sins or serious flaws. Name one! There is none. What nation has ever started as a godly nation and was able to maintain perfect godliness? There has never been one. Name one nation in the Bible that has been a sinless nation. They all have been sinful. Any nation that seeks to serve God will have sin. The same goes for a person that seeks to serve God and try to be perfect, but will still sin and have to confess it.

The problem is that we take what is happening in the world and try to fit it into the dynamics of America, as if everything revolves around America. Doing that gives us a very narrow view of prophecy. To see things prophetically accurate, we need to take what is in happening in America and fit it into the dynamics of the world. It is true that God is making changes in America, but He is also making changes in the world to set up the times of Tribulation which brings about the Second Coming of His Son Jesus Christ.

With that being said, we need to seek God and pray for America because of sin that keeps us far from God. Some of the sins that we need to confess about America are Pride, Greed, Sloth (laziness), Gluttony, Lust, Envy, Wrath (uncontrollably rage), Hatred, Jealousy and Drunkenness. That's just a few of our sins.

In our prayer for America we should (1) take notice of our confusion and shame, (2) recognize our rebellion against God, (3) admit that we have not obeyed God's voice, (4) acknowledge the disobedience that we have toward God, (5) confess that we have not prayed as we should, (6) realize that we need to turn from our iniquity in order to understand the truth, and (7) understand that America is filled with wickedness and needs a revival.

As we see all the dilemma in the world and all of the changes that have been coming to America, we know that God is moving the power of America out of the way as a superpower, in order to make the necessary international changes for the end times. We seek God for mercy and peace for America, for Israel, and for all the nations as we see God's plan unfolding in His prophetic word.

Our faith and prayers for America helps us understand the politics of the world as we stand behind the thought that:

"IT'S NOT ABOUT POLITICS, IT'S ABOUT PROPHECY"

Chapter Three
Armies in the End Times

ARMIES OF THE NORTH

Now that it is established that 'it's not about politics, it's about prophecy,' and that God used America to bring the Jewish people back to Palestine, what events will bring us closer to the Great Tribulation? What does God have to put in place before that happens?

Before the Second Coming of Christ, the Bible mentions that armies from the north will invade Israel in the future. They will probably be involved with the Battle of Armageddon in the Great Tribulation. This is part of the next great step that will be a climatic event that God has been preparing the nation of Israel for and it is mentioned in His word.

> The Bible declares this in Ezekiel 38:1-6 where it says, "Now the word of the LORD came to me, saying, "Son of man, set your face against Gog, of the land of Magog, the prince of Rosh, Meshech, and Tubal and prophesy against them... Persia, Ethiopia, and Libya are with them, all of them *with* shield and helmet; Gomer and all its troops; the house of Togarmah *from* the far north and all its troops—many people *are* with you." (NKJV)

Ezekiel 39:1-4 says, ""And you, son of man, prophesy against Gog, and say, 'Thus says the Lord God: "Behold, I *am* against you, O Gog, the prince of Rosh, Meshech, and Tubal; and I will turn you around and lead you on, bringing you up from the far north, and bring you against the mountains of Israel. Then I will knock the bow out of your left hand, and cause the arrows to fall out of your right hand. You shall fall upon the mountains of Israel, you and all your troops and the peoples who are with you." (NKJV)

RUSSIA AND ARMIES OF THE NORTH

Nations are always interested in not only governing their people but also developing an army for its protection. A huge part of politics particularly within a superpower is the size of army it can deploy. As an example, Europe that is north of Israel, has always had armies no matter which nation was the strongest on the continent.

In the invasion that is predicted there in Ezekiel 38 and 39, Russia, previously known as the USSR, will more than likely join and rely on European nations to invade Israel. That was one of the reasons for Russia's collapse in 1991. Those chapters show a group of nations involved in this military action who will all rely on each other for this invasion. Those nations may include modern day Turkey, Syria, Iraq, Iran, Ethiopia, Libya, Russia, and Gomer (Germany and other nations). They will align themselves as the armies from the nations north of Israel.

As God prepares the world for last day events that will happen, God is prophetically preparing Russia for their apparent part in this invasion of Israel in the last days. What other changes are yet in store for Russia and those other nations? If Russia is to be involved in this invasion they will have to increase their alliance and influence in European politics.

At the same time, America can remain strong but will diminish in its international influence in those areas of the world. In the future with America out of the way, this will give rise to the nations from the north on the European Continent and Asian nations from the east. They will be a part of the Great Tribulation and fight at Armageddon without significant interference from America.

As already mentioned, Russia took over the Crimea, so that northern nations can pass through the Black Sea and into the Mediterranean Sea to invade Israel at Megiddo in the northern part of their land. With God's plan and His control over the political status of the world, we can see this potential invasion developing. We realize that "It's not about Politics, it's about Prophecy."

The real problem for Israel in the future is that it will be difficult for America to defend them as they have done in the past. With the rise of other superpowers to prepare for the Great Tribulation, America's influence will change in the Middle East as its footprint of military power becomes smaller. This is happening now as God is unfolding His plan.

ARMIES OF THE EAST

The Bible also speaks of a future time when armies from the East will be involved in the major conflict of the Battle of Armageddon that is to take place in Israel. It will be a time of great distress as the Devil will do all that he can to eliminate the Jewish people, forcing them to flee out of Israel and into the wilderness.

The Bible does not say from what nations these Eastern armies will come from, but certain nations today such as China and North

Korea can fit that description. This war of the future is described in the Book of Revelation as the sixth judgment of God's wrath upon the earth.

> "Then the sixth angel poured out his bowl on the great river Euphrates, and its water was dried up, so that the way of the <u>kings from the east</u> might be prepared. And I saw three unclean spirits like frogs coming out of the mouth of the dragon, out of the mouth of the beast, and out of the mouth of the false prophet. For they are spirits of demons, performing signs, which go out to the kings of the earth and of the whole world, to gather them to <u>the battle of that great day of God Almighty</u>. "Behold, I am coming as a thief. Blessed *is* he who watches, and keeps his garments, lest he walk naked and they see his shame." And they gathered them together to the place called in Hebrew, <u>Armageddon</u>." Revelation 16:12-16 (NKJV)

Prior to this great battle, it is important to note that to ready the world, America has been involved with Asian or Eastern nations for decades such as Japan, North Korea and China. China has been brought to the forefront on the international stage as they supported North Korea's war with South Korea. It has now become an economic giant in the world community.

God has always had to raise leaders in power to make the necessary changes in the nations so that He could accomplish His purposes as it applies to the Nation of Israel and the Church. All of this is to ready Israel, the Church, and the world for the Second Coming of Jesus Christ!

In the Bible, one person whom God raised up was a vicious leader named Nebuchadnezzar. God used him to bring His chosen people Israel to Babylon as punishment for their sin and disobedience. He was a self-absorbed leader, a murderer, proud and arrogant, and who had to repent on three separate occasions. He criminally kept the Jews in captivity and would not let them go. The story of his life and leadership is recorded in the book of Daniel.

Another example in the Bible is Cyrus of Persia who was a world-ruling non-Israelite King whom God used to allowed the Jews to return to their land after the Babylonian Captivity. He did not know God, yet God called him "anointed." God said about Cyrus in Isaiah, "And why have I called you for this work? Why did I call you by name when you did not know me?" Isaiah 45:4 (NLT)

Yes, God used the leaders of the world to do His bidding. The same thing goes for America's Presidents. God has always used good or bad leaders of America and any other leaders of superpowers for that matter. God has the worldwide political situation under His control.

THE MIDDLE EAST AND THE TEMPLE

Prophetically, there have been talks between Israel and Egypt for friendship and there have been talks between Israel and the PLO about the divided land of Palestine. Those talks are a sign of a future time when agreements will be made between Israel, the Arab world, and the Antichrist. The northern and eastern nations will bring forces to the Middle East as they all will play their role over claims of political and religious rights to Palestine. The trouble in the Middle East will come to an end with the Second Coming of Christ.

In the meantime it will be very bad for Israel as it looks for help in remaining a nation and holding on to its land. The Iraq invasion after 9-11 was a war at that time that got America more deeply involved in the Middle East. It brought about the continual changes in the people and leaders of America to give them a further distaste for wars of the future in the Middle East or Europe. With that attitude, America may have a reluctance to help.

Also, the two conflicting influences of Islam and Christianity over the area of Palestine will put Israel right in the middle of everything. It gives us a picture of the conflict to come. In the end, God has a timing for these Middle East events to happen before the Millennium.

With all of these things happening, this will be a time when Israel will look to others to help her in her time of desperate need. Islam and Judaism, with the help of Christianity from around the world, will all be critically involved with the decision of the sharing of land with the Arabs in Palestine, and the building of the Temple for the Jews.

All of this tension will give rise to an ominous figure in the future that the Bible calls the Antichrist. He will be the driving force that will bring much change to the world. He will attempt to take total control of Jerusalem, which will prompt the return of Christ. The Antichrist will be involved in globalism and will have political, military, religious, oratorical, intellectual, cultural, and economic ability for world domination.

This Antichrist will arise and be the answer to what Israel is looking for. He will allow the Temple to be rebuilt, acting as a savior for its people and its land. He will make a covenant of peace with Israel and perhaps with other surrounding nations, but after that, he will demand that the world worship him. This is what the scriptures say about him:

> About the covenant of peace, Daniel 9:27 says, "And he will enter into a binding *and* irrevocable covenant

with the many for one week (seven years), but in the middle of the week he will stop the sacrifice and grain offering [for the remaining three and one-half years]; and on the wing of abominations *will come* one who makes desolate, even until the complete destruction, one that is decreed, is poured out on the one who causes the horror." (AMP)

About worshipping him, II Thessalonians 2:4 says, "He will exalt himself and defy everything that people call god and every object of worship. He will even sit in the temple of God, claiming that he himself is God." (NLT)

With Jerusalem now the capital of Israel, the Islamic Al-Aqsa Mosque will remain intact and the Jews will build their Temple near that Mosque. There is an indication in

> The Jewish people will be involved and enthralled with a new Temple, Islam will want to share the land, and Christianity will try to maintain peace.

the Bible of the Temple rebuild that will start just prior to the Great Tribulation or during it. The Jewish people will be involved and enthralled with a new Temple, Islam will want to share the land and Christianity will try to maintain the peace.

In regards to the rebuilding of the Temple in the future, here's what Revelation 11:1-2 says, "Then I was given a measuring stick, and I was told, "Go and measure the Temple of God and the altar, and count the number of worshipers. But do not measure the outer courtyard, for it has been turned over to the nations." (NLT)

What has contributed to the possibility of the building of that Temple is that there has been a disruption of international political normalcy in the Middle East and around the world and Israel is in the center of it all. As much of the world will come to rely on each other for political and economic stability, the tension in that part of the world will increase. Israel will want their Temple and the Arabs will want the recognition of their part of the land and the Temple Mount area.

Today we know that Israel is back in power as a nation, the Jewish people have support of Christianity, the Temple will be rebuilt, and the Coming of the Lord draws nigh.

Remember that we can say this phrase again and again:

"IT'S NOT ABOUT POLITICS, IT'S ABOUT PROPHECY"

Chapter Four
Birthright and Genealogy of Israel

GOD'S GUIDANCE OVER ISRAEL

Three or four centuries after the time of Christ, some Church leaders began to believe that there wasn't going to be a literal Millennium (1,000 year reign of Christ). This led some to believe that the Covenants given to Israel in the Old Testament scripture now apply to the Church. Their interpretation of those Old Testament scriptures in regards to Israel is problematic in that they look at them metaphorically (figuratively) rather than literally.

There are numerous prophecies given in the Word of God that state the blessing of God over Israel as a nation. Depending on how one interprets those passages, you can either believe that Israel as a nation will be blessed, or that there will not be a future blessing to them as a nation. You can also believe that there will be or that there will not be a final confrontation over Israel between God and the Devil.

Despite the fact that Israel was divided and disobedient, God was, and still is interested in blessing, restoring and continuing His covenant that He made with Abraham that formed a nation. That Covenant given to Abraham in Genesis 17:7-21 (KJV) will be brought to fruition and completion in the Book of Revelation when God deals with Israel to bring them back to Him.

In God's everlasting mercy to the world and an expansion of the Abrahamic Covenant, He dispatched His Son to win the world and launch the Church to bring salvation to all mankind. Christ's ministry began with the Nation of Israel and was expanded through the Apostles to bring a message to the entire world.

That did not mean that He abandoned His plans for the nation of Israel's Covenant through Abraham, but it simply was God's way of bringing a wider blessing through Israel to the Church and to peoples around the world.

In I Kings 9:5-7 (KJV), II Chronicles 7:17-20 (KJV), and Psalm 132:11-13 (KJV), it does say that if Israel remained faithful to God, someone would always sit on the throne of David and if not, they would be scattered around the world. Israel did not remain faithful and so true to God's Word, they were scattered.

> In one of those scriptures given, God said this to King Solomon, "Then I will establish the throne of your kingdom over Israel forever, as I promised David your father, saying, 'You shall not fail to have a man on the throne of Israel.' But if you or your sons at all turn from following Me, and do not keep My commandments and My statutes which I have set before you, but go and serve other gods and worship them, then I will cut off Israel from the land which I have given them; and this house which I have consecrated for My name I will cast out of My sight. Israel will be a proverb and a byword among all peoples." I Kings 9:5-7 (NKJV)

Those are verses that are both political and prophetic, but we know that prophecy transcends all politics. However, we can see why many theologians can believe that God is finished dealing with Israel as a nation. Solomon did not remain faithful to God. He disobeyed God and worshipped idols and so did his son Rehoboam. Because of that, God divided the Kingdom and it was split between the southern Kingdom of Judah and the northern Kingdom of Israel.

The northern kingdom under King Jeroboam and the southern kingdom under King Rehoboam both worshipped idols. So the kingdom in the north (10 tribes) was given the pronouncement that they were to lose their kingdom and be permanently scattered around the world as it is mentioned in I Kings 14:14-16 (KJV). Destruction soon followed the Kingdom of Judah (2 tribes) in the south and they lost their land and Temple. Hundreds of years before Christ, Judah was taken captive to Babylon. Thus God's vengeance seemed to be fulfilled.

However, it appears that God through His mercy and grace made an exception to that hard and fast rule of totally finishing off Israel as a nation. In part, it was because of God's love for King David and God's merciful extended plan of returning Israel to her former glory.

After their 70 years of captivity in Babylon, the southern tribe of Judah did return as seen in Ezra and Nehemiah. They took over the land of Israel and rebuilt their Temple again. The final destruction of Jerusalem came after the time of Christ in 70 AD, when the armies of the Roman Empire destroyed Jerusalem and the Temple. With all of that in mind, the destruction did not come without a hidden promise that came to Judah.

It would have been because of David's heart that was after God that caused God to extend His mercy to the southern tribe of Judah where David was born, and also to Benjamin who sided with Judah against the other 10 tribes (I Kings 12:21 KJV).

> About David, it states in I Samuel 13:14, "The LORD has sought for Himself a man after His own heart, and the LORD has commanded him *to be* commander over His people…" (NKJV)

Now here is the mercy of God as seen in its grandest form. This is where His grace and forgiveness comes in, and where the exception is seen. God has extended His mercy many times in the scripture even after He made an announcement of punishment. It appears like this was one of those times.

Despite all of Israel's disobedience and unfaithfulness, God did try to salvage the situation. He redirected His promise to Israel by saying that He would save one tribe for King David's sake and reject the rest. That southern kingdom was named after the tribe of Judah. The northern Nation of Israel which included the other ten tribes was scattered around the world.

> This is what God said to Solomon in I Kings 11:11, 13 "…I will surely rend the kingdom from thee, and will give it to thy servant. Howbeit <u>I will not rend away all the kingdom</u>; <u>but will give one tribe to thy son for David my servant's sake, and for Jerusalem's sake which I have chosen.</u>" (KJV)

That's a marvelous prophecy. This happened because God said that even though Israel was to collapse, Judah in the south was to be saved. This tribe was saved for the place where Christ would be born who would become the head of the Church. It was in "Bethlehem of Judaea" that both David and Jesus were from. Also, Jerusalem in Judah had become the historic place of worship for Israel and the center of Christ's ministry and birthplace of the Church.

The blessing of God upon the establishment of the Church is nothing more than profound. So is the blessing on the rebirth of Israel as a nation. The further extension of the grace of God was found in the future time when God recovered Israel for a second time. Because of the promise to Judah, Israel has been reborn and is back in their land as the news of the End Times approach.

> The blessing of God upon the establishment of the Church is nothing more than profound. So is the blessing on the rebirth of Israel as a nation.

THE BIRTHRIGHT AND THE GENEALOGY

In the Bible, the birthright was the promise from a father that he would give to his firstborn son as an inheritance, the right of authority, privilege, position and leadership in the family, and a double portion of the best of possessions. Because genealogy was part of the birthright, all of these possessions and promises would pass from firstborn son to firstborn son, and to all succeeding firstborn sons.

There were some notable exceptions to this birthright rule as well. One of those exceptions is seen in the book of I Chronicles. In this passage it says that the birthright and the genealogy were separated. Why did God do that? It's because He had a plan that included both the Nation of Israel and the Church.

> I Chronicles 5:1-2 says, "Now [we come to] the sons of Reuben the firstborn of Israel. For [Reuben] was the eldest, but because he polluted his father's couch [with Bilhah his father's concubine] his birthright was given to the sons of Joseph [favorite] son of Israel; so the genealogy is not to be reckoned according to the birthright. Judah prevailed above his brethren, and from him came the prince and leader [and

eventually the Messiah]; yet the birthright was Joseph's." (AMPC)

These promises were Prophetic. This passage says that the birthright was separated from the genealogy. That meant that the promise of the birthright privilege which gave the rights of land, possessions and ownership to the first born was given to Joseph the eleventh born which was passed down to his sons. The genealogy or lineage of the future children which was also the right of the first born, was given to Judah the fourth born and passed down to his sons. Judah was the tribe from which the Messiah came.

This is a miraculous prophecy because we know that the northern 10 tribes would be scattered to become a blessing to the nations as was promised to Abraham in Genesis 12:3 where it says, "…in you all the families of the earth shall be blessed." (NKJV)

We also know that the promise of the Messiah would come from the southern tribe of Judah just as it happened when Jesus Christ was born in "Bethlehem of Judaea." This was because of the genealogy that separated the southern kingdom of Judah from the northern kingdom of Israel that had the birthright.

This is where we understand that God does not follow "politically correctness". He fulfills two promises in one. The nations of the earth get blessed as the northern tribe of Israel is scattered among them, and the Messiah is born in Judah through whom all of the future prophecies of the Church and the Tribe of Judah were ready to be fulfilled. God does things according to His will as He turns the politics of the Old Testament birthright and genealogy rule into prophecy. All of this happens because "It's not about Politics, it's about Prophecy."

JOSEPH AND THE BIRTHRIGHT

The reason Joseph was given the birthright is revealed in Genesis 49. It says that he was fruitful and it indicates that he was bitterly attacked with envy and revenge by his brothers. Yet he remained firm and true. He triumphed over those who opposed him. He became the strength of the nation of Israel. The blessings that were promised to Joseph is vividly seen in the Book of Genesis.

> In verse 26 of Genesis chapter 49, it says, "The blessings of your father have surpassed the blessings of my ancestors up to the utmost bound of the everlasting hills; <u>may they be on the head of Joseph, and on the crown of the head of the one distinguished among his brothers</u>." (NASB)

The blessing of the birthright that was given by God to Joseph the favorite son of Jacob, was passed on to his sons Ephraim and Manasseh. The blessing to Ephraim was that the northern nation of Israel was named after him, known as Ephraim. The blessing to Manasseh was that his tribe was given land on both sides of the Jordan River and had one of the larger land areas of all the tribes.

Both the tribes of Ephraim and Manasseh were given these special blessings in the land of Israel in partial fulfillment of the Birthright that was granted to them through their father Joseph. Then after about 350 years, that northern nation was carried away from their land and scattered among the nations because of their disobedience. They were never to be seen as a nation again. God treated the northern tribe of Israel different than the southern tribe of Judah.

To help us understand how God was going to restore Israel, we must see that God had abandoned the northern nation of Israel to fulfill His promise that Israel would be scattered, but had remembered the southern nation of Judah's restoration for the End Times, and because of the promise and love for David. God's memory was intact!

JUDAH AND THE GENEALOGY

Judah was given the genealogy because his three older brothers were involved in gross and violent sin. They were passed over which meant that Judah was the next in line to receive the blessing of the genealogy prophecy.

> Genesis 49:10-11 says this about Judah, "The scepter shall not depart from Judah, nor the ruler's staff from between his feet, until Shiloh comes, and to him *shall be* the obedience of the peoples. He ties *his* foal to the vine, and his donkey's colt to the choice vine; he washes his garments in wine, and his robes in the blood of grapes." (NASB)

The coming of Shiloh means one who brings peace and tranquility as a Messiah. It can symbolize Christ and can point to one of the first times that it was said that He would come to earth. In this genealogy, Judah became the tribe that produced Jesus whose teaching brought about a following of twelve disciples who helped give birth to the Church through those teachings. Christ was the Shiloh who would come.

We are the product of those teachings and are born again into the family of God through Jesus Christ. We are with Him, and are the heir of all things through our faith in Him. The right of being "born again" as mentioned by Jesus in the third chapter of John, verses three and seven, comes as the result of the genealogy passed down to Judah, through Jesus, and unto us.

This is also a promise that even though Judah had lost its place in the role of nations, it will still have a place of obedience, judgment and restoration in the future. This is where God's prophetic plan shows that God did not have a memory lapse, nor did He forget the promise to the Jewish people that they would be restored back in their land a second time Isaiah 11:11. (KJV)

God said that one tribe was saved "For Jerusalem's sake which I have chosen." I Kings 11:13 (DARBY). The Nation of Israel is back in Palestine because of God's promise to save the tribe of Judah. This leads to a future time when Christ will reign after He returns the second time to earth.

God picked Joseph to receive the birthright and Judah to receive the genealogy. God's power of prophecy took control and changed everything to take place according to His will.

ISRAEL AND ARAB RIGHTS

That birthright privilege was eventually revived to come back to the Jewish people and it began as part of their restoration when Israel became a nation again. Restoration still belongs to them because of Jesus Christ, the Church and the nations who have stood for them. Their Covenant relationship with God will cause them to pass through the waters of tribulation as God stages His war with the Devil and the Antichrist. Then they will be permanently restored along with the Church in the New Heaven and New Earth.

Now, admittedly, there is a problem. As already stated, there were some notable exceptions to the birthright rule. In the case of the birthright that we have been talking about now, it has been said that after the time of Christ here on earth and the record of scripture, it has been difficult to prove both the biblical birthright and even the genealogy of the nation of Israel.

This is due to many years of war, migrations, mixed marriages, lack of proof of being descendent from biblical ancestors, lack of stability and security in their land over the years, and surely other factors as well.

Because of these reasons, some will say that the Jews in Palestine have no right to be there. Some say that very few Jews if any, can lay claim and proof of ancestry to the exact tribe of his or her descent. Also, it is said that Israel as a nation is simply part of a Zionist movement.

If that's the case that the Jews do not have the right to be in Palestine, then the same would have to apply to the Arab peoples who occupy much of the Middle East because they were given godly privileges as well. If they have the same lack of ancestral lineage, then they wouldn't have the right to occupy their lands either. The genealogy is hard to prove in many Middle East nations because of the difficulty in proving all of the ties with biblical ancestors.

If we reach those conclusions, it could be said that neither the Jews nor the Arab people can prove with certainty their lineage from either Isaac or Ishmael. If one was to say that the Jewish people have no right to their ancestral land, you would have to say that the Arabs have no right to their ancestral land either.

Therefore, it really isn't about the Jewish people or the Arab people having to prove their right to their ancestral lands. It isn't about the Arabs owning Palestine or Jerusalem. It isn't about the Jewish people having to prove their right to Israel or to Jerusalem. Palestine and Jerusalem doesn't belong to either of them and certainly, it doesn't belong to the Church. As already mentioned, it belongs to God!

All of the fighting and confusion is about God's land, and who has the right to possess it, nothing else! Therefore, God is using the enigma and confusion in His land to eventually bring a termination to the fighting, and a sign of Christ's coming.

Technically, it doesn't belong to Israel, or the Arabs, or the church. Therefore, realistically speaking, its God's to give to whom He wants to, and He wants those to inhabit it as He has chosen, and it's a promise that He cannot let go. It belongs to God and in Genesis God gave it to Abraham, Isaac, Jacob and their descendants. Even though they did not inhabit it continually, and even though others have inhabited it, it still belonged to their descendants forever according to Psalm 105:6-11. (KJV)

Therefore, God cannot rely on who the world says it belongs to, instead, God is using the land of Israel as a prophetic sign for the end times. He has redeemed Palestine and He has given it back to the Jewish people with the Arab nations on their backs. The Nation of Israel is reborn and in their land and God has relied on His original promise.

> When you look at prophecy you realize that Israel would be brought back to life just like the picture that iss painted for us in Ezekiel.

When you look at prophecy you realize that Israel would be brought back to life just like the picture that is painted for us in Ezekiel. These are scriptures that show that the nation of Israel will be revived in the last days despite their loss of land in the past. While some would say that the Old Testament Scriptures about Israel belong to the Church, it is not the Church that is pictured here. It is definitely the nation of Israel that Ezekiel was talking about.

> Ezekiel 37:4-5; 7; 10-14 says, "Prophesy to these bones, and say to them, 'O dry bones, hear the word of the LORD! Thus says the Lord GOD to these bones: "Surely I will cause breath to enter into you, and you shall live. So I prophesied as I was commanded; and as I prophesied, there was a noise, and suddenly a rattling; and the bones

came together, bone to bone. So I prophesied as He commanded me, and breath came into them, and they lived, and stood upon their feet, an exceedingly great army.

Then He said to me, "Son of man, these bones are the whole house of Israel. They indeed say, 'Our bones are dry, our hope is lost, and we ourselves are cut off!' Therefore prophesy and say to them, 'Thus says the Lord GOD: "Behold, O My people, I will open your graves and cause you to come up from your graves, and bring you into the land of Israel. Then you shall know that I *am* the LORD, when I have opened your graves, O My people, and brought you up from your graves. I will put My Spirit in you, and you shall live, and I will place you in your own land. Then you shall know that I, the LORD, have spoken *it* and performed *it*," says the LORD.'" (KJV)

ISRAEL'S IDENTITY

In some Old Testament modern day Covenant theology, there is a reformed or conversion idea that changes some of the Old Testament scriptures of promise. Its theological ideas of works, grace, and redemption say that the Old Testament Covenants belong to the Church and not to the Nation of Israel anymore. Of course, the Covenants and ideas of God's work in the Church are true, but they also belong to Israel as a nation. At the expense of the nation of Israel, they wrap all of God's promises of love, grace and forgiveness around the Church and not Israel.

Some of those thoughts would quote Ephesians 2:14 (KJV) that says, He "hath made both one, and hath broken down the middle wall of partition between us" which refers to Israel and the Church becoming as one. That is true. It is a great and wonderful promise. They would also quote Galatians 3:28 (KJV) that says "There is neither Jew nor Greek, there is neither bond nor free," and that we "are all one in Christ Jesus." That scripture is definitely true as well, but it doesn't say that He means that Israel has lost their identity as a nation. It's not the complete picture.

That same verse in Galatians 3:28 (KJV) also says, "there is neither male nor female: for ye are all one in Christ Jesus." Male and female of course are one in Christ but they keep their identity. They are not one at the expense of the identity of the other. Spiritually, they have wonderful promises that apply to each of them as two separate parts of marriage in Christ. Again, they both keep their identity and wonderful promises as male and female that make them unique.

Israel and the Church are one in Christ as well but they keep their identity which makes them also unique. There are wonderful promises made to the Church but there are also wonderful promises that still belong to the nation of Israel. Just like the male and female, they are not one at the expense of one or the other.

Now it is true that Israel failed God many times and He abandoned northern Israel as a nation and the Southern nation of Judah lost everything after the crucifixion of Christ. Yet God has still promised that Israel would be recovered. His total rejection of His chosen people did not happen to the nation of Israel as a whole but only to Israel in the north (I Kings 14:14-16 KJV; II Kings 17:18-23 KJV). It did not apply to Judah in the south (II Kings 8:19 KJV; Isaiah 54:7-8 KJV; Jeremiah 31:31-37 KJV; 33:24-26 KJV). The door was left wide open for the future of Israel.

> II Kings 8:19 says, "Yet the LORD would not destroy Judah, for the sake of His servant David, as He

promised him to give a lamp to him *and* his sons forever." (NKJV)

Jeremiah 33:24-26 says, "Have you not considered what these people have spoken, saying, 'The two families which the LORD has chosen, He has also cast them off'? Thus they have despised my people, as if they should no more be a nation before them. "Thus says the LORD: 'If My covenant *is* not with day and night, *and if* I have not appointed the ordinances of heaven and earth, then I will cast away the descendants of Jacob and David My servant, *so* that I will not take *any* of his descendants *to be* rulers over the descendants of Abraham, Isaac, and Jacob. For I will cause their captives to return, and will have mercy on them.'" (NKJV)

Also, the controversy of Romans nine through eleven is that there are some who say that those three chapters refer to Israel and others that say they refer to the Church. In actuality they refer to both Israel and the Church because while the Church is the "elect" in those chapters, Israel is also the "elect" because they can be grafted in again (Romans 11:23) (KJV) and they are referred to as the "elect" (Romans 11:28). (KJV)

You may ask why all of this? Why do you make reference to both Israel and the Church? Because God has these eternal and prophetic purposes in mind in which He had a plan that included redemption. It began with just one couple in the Garden of Eden and ended with redemption for the entire world.

We know that in the future there will be a time when the Arab world will be united with the Jewish world, serving Christ. Even though the Arab world strongly endorses Islam, they will eventually come to Christ. It will more than likely be at a time when during the Millennium, Christ will rule the world with a rod of iron.

> Romans 14:11 says, "For it is written, as I live, saith the Lord, every knee shall bow to me, and every tongue shall confess to God." (KJV)

There is a prophetic picture of how the Arab world and the Jewish world will work together at that time when together they believe in the one true God, the Father of the Lord Jesus Christ. They will be a group of three nations that will work together and cooperate with Christ at that future time. The whole idea is that Israel has to be rebirthed in order for God to work together with these other nations and bring the rest of the events of the future to completion.

> Isaiah 19:23-25 says, "In that day there will be a highway from <u>Egypt</u> to <u>Assyria</u>. The Assyrians will go to Egypt and the Egyptians to Assyria. The Egyptians and Assyrians will worship together. In that day <u>Israel will be the third, along with Egypt and Assyria</u>, a blessing on the earth. The Lord Almighty will bless them, saying, <u>Blessed be Egypt my people, Assyria my handiwork, and Israel my inheritance</u>." (NIV)

Even though politics does not understand the fate of the Jewish and Arab people and the heritage and right to their ancestral lands, God is the one who will dictate the future of these people. He is the one who will set things up in the world before the Second Coming of Jesus Christ.

Politics does not understand this, but that doesn't matter because:

"IT'S NOT ABOUT POLITICS, IT'S ABOUT PROPHECY"

Chapter Five
Israel and the Church

ISRAEL'S OPPORTUNITY

There are numerous prophetic messages and promises given to Israel that have to be taken literally in regards to the End-Times. There is a plan and there are scriptures in God's Word that unmistakably gives the opportunity for hope to Israel in the last days. The Bible says,

1. **That Israel would face tribulation in the latter days** – "In your distress <u>when all these things happen to you in the latter days</u>, if you return to the LORD your God and obey him (for he is a merciful God), he will not let you down or destroy you, for he cannot forget the covenant with your ancestors that he confirmed by oath to them." (Deuteronomy 4:30-31 NET)

2. **That there is still a Covenant with Abraham, Isaac, and Jacob** – "He hath remembered his covenant forever, <u>the word which he commanded to a thousand generations. Which covenant he made with Abraham, and his oath unto Isaac; and confirmed the same unto Jacob for a law, and to Israel for an everlasting covenant</u>: Saying, unto thee will I give the land of Canaan, the lot of your inheritance." (Psalm 105:8-11 KJV)

3. **That God would not abandon the seed of Israel** – "Thus says the LORD, which giveth <u>the sun for a light by day, and the ordinances of the moon and of the stars for a light by night</u>, which divides the sea when the waves thereof roar; The LORD of hosts is his name: <u>If those ordinances depart from before me, says the LORD, then the seed of Israel also shall cease from being a nation before me forever.</u>" (Jeremiah 31:35-36 – KJV)

No doubt about it, these scriptures belong to a physical nation of Israel. Long ago in that scripture of Deuteronomy 4:30-31 (NET) God pointedly talked about the fact that the nation of Israel being in existence at that time would pass through a time of great Tribulation. He wasn't talking about the Church that didn't even exist yet.

The Scripture in Psalm 105:8-11 (KJV) says that God gave His word to Abraham, Isaac, and Jacob that the land of Canaan would be theirs for a thousand generations which indicates an innumerable calculation. In this passage, God was not speaking about Israel metaphorically, He was speaking about a physical inheritance in the land of Canaan.

In the Scripture of Jeremiah 31:35-36 (KJV) God was going to hold the sun, moon and stars in the universe accountable in keeping track of Israel. God said that His ordinances would give testimony that He would not forget the seed or the physical beginning of Israel in respect to their nation being instituted by God and being remembered forever.

ISRAEL'S SECOND RECOVERY

Statements have been made about the Nation of Israel that their recovery from exile in Babylon was fully accomplished in the Old Testament and that there is no need for a second return in the future.

One statement that I have recently read says that there is no prophecy in the Bible that mentions a second return after that Babylonian exile hundreds of years before the time of Christ.

Nothing could be further from the truth! Isaiah was a prophet before the exile of the Nation of Israel into Babylon and he died about one hundred years or so prior to that time. The first return of the Jews from exile hadn't even happened yet and Isaiah was talking about a second return. Some had been exiled to Babylon, others fled to Egypt while thousands remained in Judah but God had a future return in mind.

In Isaiah eleven, verse one (KJV) it mentions a time when there will be peace. In that chapter he talks about an individual born from the family tree of Jesse, the father of King David. This person who was to come would have the Spirit of God upon Him and would judge righteously.

It will be at a future time of peace when the earth will be full of the knowledge of the Lord. It will be a sign or a signal to the peoples of the world and will bring a time of rest that will be glorious for everyone. That person mentioned in Isaiah eleven is largely looked upon as the Messiah.

> The recovery of Israel for the second time is mentioned in Isaiah 11:11-13, where is says, "And in that day the Lord shall again lift up His hand a <u>second time</u> to recover (acquire and deliver) the remnant of His people which is left, from Assyria, from Lower Egypt, from Pathros [Upper Egypt], from Ethiopia, from Elam [in Persia], from Shinar [Babylonia], from Hamath [in Upper Syria], and from the countries bordering on the [Mediterranean] Sea. And He will raise up a signal for the nations

and will assemble the outcasts of Israel and will gather together the dispersed of Judah from the four corners of the earth. The envy *and* jealousy of Ephraim also shall depart, and they who vex *and* harass Judah from outside *or* inside shall be cut off; Ephraim shall not envy Judah, and Judah shall not vex *and* harass Ephraim." (AMPC)

Some people really do believe that there are no promises left for the Nation of Israel and that the Jews can only be saved through the Church just like anyone else. Of course, Jewish people can be saved, but the Old Testament Eschatological prophetic promises are to be taken literally to represent the Nation of Israel. Again, Jewish people are being saved, but we cannot accept the conclusion that God is finished with them as a nation.

Yes, God indicates that the promise to Israel is that they would be brought back at two separate times. The first time was after their captivity in Babylon. They were restored during the days of Ezra and Nehemiah about 500 years before the time of Christ. This was after the command by Cyrus the Persian king that Jewish people could return to the land of Palestine. The second time was in 1948 AD after WW II.

CHRIST RULES OVER THE CHURCH

In the meantime, right in the middle of when Israel lost their place in the heart of God, and when He would eventually restore them in the future, the Church was birthed. The gospel was to be propagated around the world through His Son Jesus Christ.

Right in the middle of when Israel lost their place in the heart of God, and when He would eventually restore them in the future, the Church was birthed.

The Book of Revelation tells us that since the birth of the Church, Christ is now sitting on His throne in Heaven and that He is in the midst of the throne. Not long before the destruction of Jerusalem in 70 AD, He ascended into Heaven and He has been ruling over the Church from heaven since that time.

> The Church of Laodicea Revelation 3:21 shows us a picture of Christ. It says, "To him who overcomes I will grant to sit with me on <u>my throne</u>, as I also overcame and sat down with My Father on His throne." (NKJV)

> Revelation 5:6 says, "And I looked, and behold, in the <u>midst of the throne</u> and of the four living creatures, and in the midst of the elders, stood a Lamb as though it had been slain, having seven horns and seven eyes, which are the seven Spirits of God sent out into all the earth." (NKJV)

Notice in that passage of Revelation 3:21 that Christ told the Church of Laodicea that if they would be overcomers, they could sit with Him on His throne. Of course, that was not only for the Church at that time but it can be applied to all believers in the Church of any time in the future. We also know that Christ is already sitting on the throne of our hearts because He lives within us. If He lives within us and we sanctify and dedicate ourselves to Him, we can then believe that He then has a special place in our hearts.

> I Peter 3:15 describes how the Lord should rule in our hearts when it says, "But sanctify the Lord God in your hearts, and always *be* ready to *give* a defense to everyone who asks you a reason for the hope that is in you, with meekness and fear." (NKJV)

Christ's rule is seen in the announcement by the Angel Gabriel to Mary just before her child was conceived by the Holy Spirit. Gabriel said to her about Jesus' birth in Luke 1:32-33:

> "He will be great, and will be called the Son of the Highest; and the Lord God will give Him the throne of His father David. And He will reign over the house of Jacob forever, and of His kingdom there will be no end." (NKJV)

Christ has been spiritually ruling in the hearts of believers for the past two thousand years and will also rule physically in the future during the Millennium. This is understood because of the separation between the Birthright and Genealogy seen in the previous chapter. The Birthright is a blessing to the nations of the world, and the Genealogy is a blessing to the nation of Israel.

In Romans 11:24 (KJV), God said that Israel can be grafted in again. The context is referring to Israel as a nation. In verse 25 (KJV) of that same chapter, it mentions the word "mystery." The word "mystery" in the Greek is mü-stā'-rē-on. It is a derivative of a word which means "to shut the mouth" as if one is keeping a secret. It simply means a "secret" or "hidden purpose." The secret and mystery is there but is revealed by God to all who would receive it.

A careful study of adoption and election by God reveals that both the Church and the Nation of Israel are referenced, and not just the Jewish people being saved through the Church. The hidden purpose is that both Israel and the Church will be saved. This is what it says:

> Romans 11:24-25 says, "For if thou wert cut out of the olive tree which is wild by nature and wert grafted contrary to nature into a good olive tree: <u>how much more shall these, which be the natural</u>

branches be grafted into their own olive tree?
For I do not wish you to be ignorant, brethren,
of this <u>mystery,</u> that ye may not be wise in your
own conceits, that <u>blindness in part is happened</u>
<u>to Israel, until the fullness of the nations be come</u>
<u>in;.</u>" (Darby)

It is difficult to see how God can remove Israel as a nation because
of their sin, but yet give them the promise and understanding that
they would be brought back as a nation again. It is hard for many to
understand that, especially for those who say that the Old Testament
Covenants that belong to Israel, now belong to the Church.

One huge promise that we can rely on is what God's word says in
the Book of Romans about the irrevocable Election of the Nation
of Israel and the Election of the Church through God's mercy.
We discover that there are verses in Romans that tell us about the
election of the Church, but also that the rejection of Israel is not
final. God still has a plan for them.

> This is what Romans 11:26-29 says about <u>the</u>
> <u>Nation of Israel,</u> "And so <u>all Israel will be saved,</u> as
> it is written: 'The Deliverer will come out of Zion,
> And He will turn away ungodliness from Jacob; For
> this *is* My covenant with them, When I take away
> their sins.' Concerning the gospel *they are* enemies
> for your sake, but concerning the election they are
> beloved for the sake of the fathers. <u>For the gifts and</u>
> <u>the calling of God are irrevocable.</u>" (NKJV)

> This is what Romans 11:30-33 says about <u>the</u>
> <u>Church,</u> "For as you were once disobedient to
> God, yet have now obtained mercy through their
> disobedience, even so these also have now been

disobedient, that through the mercy shown you they also may obtain mercy. For God has committed them all to disobedience, <u>that He might have mercy on all. Oh, the depth of the riches both of the wisdom and knowledge of God! How unsearchable *are* His judgments and His ways past finding out!</u>" (NKJV)

Who can understand that kind of mercy and that kind of wisdom that would bring about a plan like that? With the nation of Israel now recovered and the Church in place, the only thing that we know is that at each critical time in history, God has always had a person, a people, a nation or a Church that He could work with. His plan of saving His creation from the evil work of the Devil has always been in play. His message was brought about in so many different ways to so many different people who could work with Him to bring Him honor and glory.

The reason for the rebirth of Israel as a nation is so that each of us in the Church could understand that the Second Coming of Christ will happen sooner than we expect.

The Church must understand that:

"IT'S NOT ABOUT POLITICS, IT'S ABOUT PROPHECY"

Chapter Six
Nations of the World

BIBLICAL NATIONS OF THE WORLD

In order to understand that "It's not about politics, it's about prophecy," you have to realize that God moves the nations to do His will, not for political reasons but for prophetic reasons. God has always and still is in control of the nations.

He uses His strength and ability to accomplish the culmination of events here on earth before the Coming of the Lord. He is moving things forward toward the future New Heaven and New earth. He knows how to use the governments of different nations and their activity and their behavior.

God has always had a message about the nations of the world. He spoke through the prophet Habakkuk concerning the southern Nation of Judah that was being punished by its enemies. The prophet had a great burden. He was complaining about the injustice that was being done to the nation. God had a reply for him. It was a powerful pronouncement from God as an encouragement to the people. It is something that could be applied to our time.

> Habakkuk 1:4-5 says, "For the wicked surround
> the righteous; therefore, justice becomes perverted.

[The LORD replied,] Look among the nations! See! Be astonished! Wonder! For I am doing something in your days—you would not believe it if you were told." (AMP)

God had to bring the Nation of Israel back to the land of Palestine but He had to do it His way and in His time. God has done all of this through prophecy and not because of politics. He places Himself over the leaders of the world. He uses world situations and power struggles to change things for His glory and for the Second Coming of His Son Jesus Christ. As already mentioned, He uses prophets to announce His plans and then He puts them in place.

God is trying to reveal something like that today. As we pray about the nations and see the actions of many that have drifted far away from God, we have faith to realize and believe that miracles and wonders can be revealed in our time as well. God is indeed preparing the world today for an event that is clearly revealed in the Book of Revelation. The coming together of nations that are inspired by the Devil will be a last ditch effort to undermine the works of God.

All superpower nations have had some influence over Israel, whether for good or for evil. As far as Israel is concerned, God has always used the nations of the world to further His plan. All of this happened because of Israel's disobedience and willful sin. They became a byword (mock, ridicule) among the nations (Deuteronomy 28:37). (KJV) Despite all of that, Israel still remains God's covenant people from the book of Genesis to the book of Revelation.

> Israel still remains God's covenant people from the book of Genesis to the book of Revelation.

Again, God always uses Superpowers to accomplish His will and way in prophecy. God's step by step master plan brought about the strength of the superpower nations that have had a major impact on Israel. Following are the nations that God has used:

(1) **Egypt** tortured and enslaved Jacob's family after they joined Joseph in that land. Moses was picked by God to lead them out of Egypt through the Red Sea to occupy Palestine in order to establish their own nation. That was a move by God for the prophetic purpose of establishing the Jewish people as a nation in the Promised Land.

(2) **Assyria** invaded the northern Kingdom of Israel and took their people out of their land and scattered them all over the world. Kings of Assyria fought against the northern Kingdom after Israel was divided into the two kingdoms of Israel and Judah. The aftermath of those invasions prophetically fulfilled I Kings 14:14-16 (KJV) and also II Kings 17:18-23 (KJV), which say that the northern Kingdom of Israel would be rejected and scattered.

(3) **Babylon** took the southern Kingdom of Judah out of their land and into captivity for 70 years. Babylon continued to persecute them as seen by their difficulties. Babylon then had to be destroyed. They would never have allowed the Jews to be free so they could return again to their homeland.

(4) **Persia** was the nation that invaded and destroyed Babylon in battle and allowed the Jews to return to the land of Israel after 70 years of captivity. This return happened because of the prophetic edict of Cyrus the King in II Chronicles 36:22-23 (KJV), and Isaiah 45:1-5 (KJV). He was the one who made the pronouncement that allowed the Children of Israel to return.

(5) **Greece** invaded Jerusalem between the Old and New Testaments, killing many of its people and destroyed much property after Alexander the Great's kingdom was divided after his death. They

committed sacrilege by offering an unclean animal on the altar of the Temple.

(6) **Rome** severely persecuted the Jews for years during and after the time of Christ. It was the empire that played a major role in the crucifixion of Christ. The Jews did not realize that they were speaking a prophetic word when they said at Christ's crucifixion, "His blood be on us and on our children." After those words, Israel lost their Temple and land in less than 40 years.

These superpower nations mentioned in the Bible have had a prophetic impact and influence in God's guidance over the nation of Israel. Some of their influence was for the good of Israel and some of it was for their punishment.

Mostly because of God's plan for Israel, these nations were used by God to bring correction or aid to the nation. Each great superpower had a powerful leader or series of leaders that helped their empire create a lasting influence over Israel and the world.

OTHER NATIONS OF THE WORLD

It's little wonder that even nations that continued after the time of the Bible would have some kind of relationship with Israel as well. Some of those other nations that are not mentioned in the Bible that have had an impact on the land of Israel have been the Ottoman Empire, the Holy Roman Empire, the British Empire, and the United States of America.

(1) **The Holy Roman Empire** was called so because of the blessing of the Church. The Church wanted to win the Holy Land back from Muslim control. The Popes helped initiate the Crusades that took place during the 11th, 12th, and 13th Centuries. They were not inspired by God because it wasn't His time to re-establish the Nation

of Israel. In the future, God wanted to win Palestine back on His terms in order to recreate the Nation of Israel.

(2) **The Ottoman (Islamic) Empire** took over the failing Christian Roman/Byzantine Empire between the 14th and early 20 centuries and ruled in Palestine. To prepare for the Jews return, the Ottoman Empire was dissolved at the end of WW I after they sided with Germany and Austria-Hungary toward the end of the war. They were defeated and lost control of Palestine. Then Britain and The United States allowed the Jews to return to the land of Israel in great numbers.

THE GERMANIC DIVISION OF THE ROMAN EMPIRE

The blessings of the Church on the emperors began just prior to the Crusades. It started a spiritual demonic union between the carnal leadership of the Empire and the Church. It was a fateful union that led to the First, Second, and Third Reich. That union eventually brought disaster for the Jewish people but set the stage for their eventual return to the Holy Land.

In 962 AD, the Pope crowned Otto the Great as emperor of the Holy Roman Empire. He was German, and his coronation is usually considered to be the **First Reich**.

In time, Germany was weakened. Otto Von Bismarck, a great genius in Europe's history, united the German division of the Empire which was the **Second Reich** ruled by the Kaisers, or Emperors. It lasted from 1871 until 1918. After their loss in WW I, they became a democracy.

That union was in a chain of German emphasis and leadership that eventually led to the most hated man of the 20th Century, the murderous Adolf Hitler of the **Third Reich**. In 1933, Adolf Hitler was appointed Chancellor of Germany after which he cast off democracy and took over as dictator. He invaded other countries, and allowed the beginning of the murder of millions of people. Hitler was defeated in 1945 by Allied forces.

The union of the Church and the Empire sealed the fate of six million Jews who were going to be murdered in WW II. Somehow God allowed this horrible event called the holocaust that in the human mind is totally despicable and unacceptable. This however, allowed the Jews to form their nation again.

(3) The British Empire after the end of WW I, recognized the right of the Jewish people to have a home in their ancestral land of Palestine and was given control of it. However, after WW II they did not want Israel to have sovereignty. They opposed them and fought against the dividing of Israel into Arab and Jewish states. They voted against Israel being admitted into the United Nations after Israel became a nation.

(4) The United States of America as already covered was raised as a superpower to replace the British Empire whose leadership began to change toward the establishment of Israel as a nation. America had a major role in helping the nation of Israel return to Palestine. It has been a supporter of Israel over the years.

America has been there for Israel with the understanding that they had a right to be in the land of their ancestry. Now Israel is a sign from God that He is ready to bring closure to the many difficulties of their past existence.

Unfortunately, the demonic union between the Church and the Empires which led to the Third Reich, will in the future lead to the Apostate Church which is described in Revelation 17 as a woman prostitute. She is riding on the back of a beast believed to be the Antichrist, who will bring much distress and fear in the last days. This union between the woman and the beast will be a powerful evil entity of religion and politics but the Antichrist will eventually turn on the Church during that time as seen in the sixteenth verse of that same chapter. This is what it says about the woman's adornment in Revelation 17:4-6:

> "The woman was arrayed in purple and scarlet, and adorned with gold and precious stones and pearls, having in her hand a golden cup full of abominations and the filthiness of her fornication. And on her forehead a name *was* written: MYSTERY, BABYLON THE GREAT THE MOTHER OF HARLOTS AND OF THE ABOMINATIONS OF THE EARTH. I saw the woman, drunk with the blood of the saints and with the blood of the martyrs of Jesus. And when I saw her, I marveled with great amazement." (NKJV)

God has used each of the nations throughout history to bring about His judgment upon the people He has loved, but also to show that His everlasting love and mercy can be and was extended to those very same people. Israel is back in their land showing God's love for their total salvation as a nation before the return of Jesus Christ. The timing of that love that He has toward Israel is a picture of the love that He has for the world as well.

> His timetable is different than ours in that we know that "one day is with the Lord as a thousand years, and a thousand years as one day" (II Peter 3:8). (KJV)

God has patience for His people. Therefore, to understand the power of politics that all of these nations have had over the nation of Israel, we come to the conclusion that:

"IT'S NOT ABOUT POLITICS, IT'S ABOUT PROPHECY"

Chapter Seven
Covenants and Sovereignty of God

THE COVENANTS OF GOD

The covenants of the Old Testament were given to Israel as a nation and because of that, God will bring them salvation. The scripture in Jeremiah 31:31 (AMPC) where God says that He would make "a new Covenant with the house of Israel" refers to the nation of Israel.

> Jeremiah 31:31-34 says, "Behold, the days are coming, says the Lord, when <u>I will make a new covenant with the house of Israel and with the house of Judah</u>, not according to the covenant which I made with their fathers in the day when I took them by the hand to bring them out of the land of Egypt, my covenant which they broke, although I was their Husband, says the Lord. But this is the covenant which I will make with the house of Israel: After those days, says the Lord, I will put my law within them, and on their hearts will I write it; and I will be their God, and they will be my people. And they will no more teach each man his neighbor and each man his brother, saying, Know the Lord, for they will all know me [recognize, nderstand, and be acquainted with me], from the least of them to

the greatest, says the Lord. For I will forgive their iniquity, and I will [seriously remember their sin no more." (AMPC)

As indicated also in Hebrews 8:7-13 (NKJV), He will renew that Covenant with Israel. In part of that scripture in Hebrews 8 it says in verses 8-10,

> Because finding fault with them, He says: "Behold, the days are coming, says the LORD, when I will make a new covenant with the house of Israel and with the house of Judah— not according to the covenant that I made with their fathers in the day when I took them by the hand to lead them out of the land of Egypt; because they did not continue in My covenant, and I disregarded them, says the LORD. For this *is* the covenant that I will make with the house of Israel after those days, says the LORD: I will put my laws in their mind and write them on their hearts; and I will be their God, and they shall be my people." (NKJV)

Those scriptures are definitely talking about the Nation of Israel because of the reference to both the house of Israel and the house of Judah. God has a plan for Israel as a nation in Palestine as well a plan for the Church around the world.

The renewed Covenant is still in force. If God would renew that Covenant with a group of people and would leave Israel out of the equation, then He is reneging on His original promise to Israel receiving a new Covenant. Both Israel and Judah were promised this renewal so that God could always keep them as a guide or a beacon of light of salvation to the rest of the world. This promise extends from the scriptures written in Jeremiah and Hebrews and extend into the Millennium.

This was a duel prophecy. Israel was part of this renewal of restoration when it was scattered as a blessing to all of the other nations of the world through the Church. Judah was a part of it as well when God said He would not tear apart all of the kingdom (I Kings 11:11-13 KJV). That promise of not taking away all of the kingdom would be an unconditional promise to the nation of Israel about their restoration and return to Palestine which is revealed in Deuteronomy 30:1-10 (KJV). God satisfied both His command to scatter Israel and His desire to restore Israel.

> Israel was part of this renewal of restoration when it was scattered as a blessing to all of the other nations of the world. Judah was a part of it as well when God said He would not tear apart all of the kingdom.

The basic Covenants of God are the Covenants with Adam, Noah, Abraham, Palestine, Moses, and David. There are three unconditional Covenants which are the Abrahamic, Palestinian, and Davidic Covenants. There is one conditional Covenant which is the Mosaic Covenant. There are two neutral Covenants which are the ones to Adam and to Noah that are not to a certain group of people but instead to a wide range of people.

The following defines the three unconditional Covenants. Following are those Covenants that are a prophecy that God will always honor the promises to the nation of Israel.

1. The Covenant with Abraham – This Covenant was a promise to Abraham to make his name great. His seed would bless the nations of the world, and God would make of him a great nation. This unconditional Covenant was sealed with the sign of circumcision (Romans 4:11). (KJV)

2. The Palestinian Covenant – If Israel disobeyed God, they were told that God would scatter them around the world. Part of that Covenant was that God would also restore them and bring them back to their land (Deuteronomy 30:1-10). (KJV) This restoration happened twice, once after the Babylonian captivity and then again in 1948.

3. The Covenant with David – God said that his kingdom and family line would last forever. The tribe of Judah was saved for David and Jesus was born from that same tribe. The line of Judah led to the church and the Book of Revelation reveals that both Israel and the Church will share in the New Heaven and New Earth.

These unconditional Covenants gave assurance that the nation of Israel would always be in the mind of God, saved, punished, and then restored at the appropriate time. These Covenants insure the fact that God's chosen people will always be used by God to deliver a message to the world about His prophetic plans. The following steps are promises to Israel and the Church that involves them in eternity.

ORDER OF THE PROPHETIC STEPS TO ETERNITY

1. A Covenant promise to the nation of Israel which says that they would be a blessing to all the nations of the world.

2. A Covenant promise to Judah that God's servant David would always be a lamp before Him in Jerusalem.

3. Salvation for every man, woman, and child who believe in Him through a broadened plan of blessing that is called the Church.

4. The Rapture of the believers.

5. Horrific events of the Great Tribulation that lead to Armageddon in a final standoff between God and Satan to rescue the covenant that God had with the nation of Israel.

6. Crowns and rewards given to Christians at the Judgment seat of Christ.
7. The marriage of the Church to Jesus Christ.
8. The Millennial reign of Christ on the earth with a rod of iron with Israel and the Church.
9. The renovation of the earth by fire.
10. A New Heaven and New Earth recreated by God for Israel and the Church.
11. All of eternity spent with God.

The calling and reference of both Israel and the Church in the End Times is why we place an emphasis of Israel and the Church as being two entities that God will use in the last days. It is also why we believe in the Rapture of the Church so that God can deal with the nation of Israel separately from the Church, so that along with the Church they can reign with Him in eternity.

While God was building the Church, Israel was gone because they were scattered throughout the centuries, blessing all of the other nations. When the Church is Raptured, God deals with Israel during the Great Tribulation to restore His Covenant relationship with them.

THE SOVEREIGNTY OF GOD

There is much that can be said about the sovereignty and omnipotence of God. It is important to believe in the sovereignty of God because of the plan that He has in designing a people to be with Him for all of eternity. His work is well thought out and is not haphazard, nor is it given over to a whim or chance. Webster's Dictionary defines sovereignty as "supreme power, freedom from external control or controlling influence." That's our Sovereign God!

The Sovereignty of God means:

1. All things are under God's rule and control.
2. Nothing happens without God's permission.
3. God turns bad into good.
4. All things lead to and happen within God's will.
5. God has the power and right to govern all things, without exception.

Man makes decisions that affect things in his everyday life but all things in finality and totality fall into the hands of the living God. Even when things that are bad or work contrary to the will of God, He knows how to correct things and even make bad things help re-direct our lives. He has more superiority in matters of sovereignty than the Devil or man.

> "Do we believe in the sovereignty of man, the sovereignty of the Devil, the sovereignty of God, or perhaps there is no sovereignty at all?"

This leads us to the question, "Do we believe in the sovereignty of man, the sovereignty of the Devil, the sovereignty of God, or perhaps there is no sovereignty at all?" It cannot be the sovereignty of man because man would have the final say with our lives and not have to answer to God. It cannot be the sovereignty of the Devil because he then can overthrow God as he (Lucifer) tried to do in Isaiah 14:12-15 (KJV). It cannot be no sovereignty or we may all end up believing that there is no control over what happens with our world. It would be similar to Deism which is non-interference by the Creator in the laws that govern the universe.

Our conclusion has to be a belief in the sovereignty of God which helps us to understand that God has absolute and final control of all things that happen in Heaven and on earth. During our lifetime and finally in the end of time, all things flow into him for His approval or dismissal.

When bad or evil things happen to us God can use them to bring about good things in our lives because God is sovereign over both good and evil (Isaiah 45:7 KJV) and He can use either one or both for His own glory and power.

> As it says in Romans 8:28, "And we know that all things work together for good to those who love God, to those who are the called according to *His* purpose." (NKJV)

Give some further thought to the following scriptures:

> Daniel 4:35 says, "All the inhabitants of the earth are accounted as nothing, but He does according to His will in the host of heaven and among the inhabitants of earth; and no one can ward off His hand or say to Him, What have You done?" (NASB)

> Isaiah 43:13 says, "Even from eternity I am He, and there is none who can deliver out of my hand; I act and who can reverse it?" (NASB)

> Job 42:1-2 says, "Then Job answered the Lord and said, I know that you can do all things, and that no thought *or* purpose of yours can be restrained." (AMP)

God's power and sovereignty can especially be seen in Isaiah 46:5, 9-10:

> To whom will ye liken me, and make me equal, and compare me that we may be like? Remember the

things of old: for I am God, and there is none else; I am God, and there is none like me, declaring the end from the beginning, and from ancient times the things that are not yet done, saying, my counsel shall stand, and I will do all my pleasure." (KJV)

The following scripture is for our edification and the hope of God always with us for encouragement and grace:

II Corinthians 4:8-11, 16-18 says, "We are hard-pressed on every side, yet not crushed; *we are* perplexed, but not in despair; persecuted, but not forsaken; struck down, but not destroyed—always carrying about in the body the dying of the Lord Jesus, that the life of Jesus also may be manifested in our body. For we who live are always delivered to death for Jesus' sake, that the life of Jesus also may be manifested in our mortal flesh. Therefore we do not lose heart. Even though our outward man is perishing, yet the inward *man* is being renewed day by day. For our light affliction, which is but for a moment, is working for us a far more exceeding *and* eternal weight of glory, while we do not look at the things which are seen, but at the things which are not seen. For the things which are seen *are* temporary, but the things which are not seen *are* eternal." (NKJV)

AUTHORITIES IN THE BIBLE

There are only two dominant authorities or powers in the Bible, God and the Devil. All other authorities and all powers come under the authority of God and the Devil. You can't talk about God without talking about the Devil and you can't talk about the Devil without talking about God. The creative power of God can be seen in Colossians 1:15-19:

> "The Son is the image of the invisible God, the firstborn over all creation. For in him all things were created: things in heaven and on earth, visible and invisible, whether thrones or powers or rulers or authorities; all things have been created through him and for him. He is before all things, and in him all things hold together. And he is the head of the body, the church; he is the beginning and the firstborn from among the dead, so that in everything he might have the supremacy. For God was pleased to have all his fullness dwell in him." (NIV)

Even the Devil is under the authority and power of God because at the end of time he will be cast into the lake of fire, eternally separated from God. In the meantime while the struggle over the earth continues in the present, even the Devil has a level of ruling authority over evil powers as we understand it in Ephesians 6:12 were it says:

> "For our struggle is not against flesh and blood, but against the rulers, against the authorities, against the powers of this dark world and against the spiritual forces of evil in the heavenly realms." (NIV)

When you read the Old Testament, you see the faith of the Patriarchs and the Prophets, many of whom wrote those sacred passages. You also read about the Kings who ruled over Israel and the kings and peoples of all the other nations of the world. However, God had final authority.

In the New Testament you see the faith of Christ, the Disciples, the believers and all of the authors who saw Christ and/or who wrote about Him. You can also see the horrible political deeds of the Roman Empire who ruled much of the world at the time and who helped put Christ to death. God had the final authority.

This is the empire that also confronted Paul and the other Disciples, many of whom had to give their lives for the cause of Christ. Many believers were a part of the New Testament time as a record of the early deeds of the Church were recorded. You can see both the religious and political influence in the entire New Testament. God had final authority.

God is strong and all powerful. He is in control of all things in Heaven and on earth. Everything that happens on the earth serves as a message for us that we must be ready for the Second Coming of Jesus Christ.

The Rapture of the Church is the next big event that is to take place that will affect the future of the Church and the world. All things that will happen during the Great Tribulation, the Millennial Reign of Jesus Christ on the earth, and in the New Heaven and New Earth to come, has a prophetic purpose and understanding for us today and in the future.

Keep this in mind, "If you want to understand what God is going to do in the future, simply find out what He's done in the past" because history repeats itself.

Finally, what is best to remember is:

"IT'S NOT ABOUT POLITICS, IT'S ABOUT PROPHECY"

Current Events Leading up to Armageddon

In our understanding of the future of prophecy, the horrific time of the Great Tribulation will definitely be a time of bringing the Jews to a complete understanding as to who Christ is. This time of climax of the difficulties in the world, is to bring them to a return of the Covenant relationship that they have with God.

1. Jerusalem as the Capital of Israel will lead to sharing the land of Palestine. The Jews will get their temple and the Arabs will get their share of Palestine.
2. Christ will come for the Church at the start of the Great Tribulation and will come upon the world at the end of the Great Tribulation because His return is a two-fold blessing.
3. Christ will return to fight in Armageddon at the end of the Great Tribulation because the nations have divided His land – Joel 3:1-2. (KJV)
4. Russia took over the Crimea in the Black Sea in 2014. Armies from the North can travel from the Crimea through the Bosporus Strait into the Mediterranean Sea and invade Israel as Armies of the North – Ezekiel 37-38. (KJV) A sign of the times.

5. The President's dealings with both Korea's is a signal of a coming invasion of Armies of the East in Revelation 16:12-16 (KJV). Korea may possibly be a part of those armies.
6. Nations think they are doing the right thing by opposing or wanting to kill and destroy Israel, but they do not know Christ or the Father – John 16:1-3 (KJV).

Rapture of the Church Fulfilling Prophecy

The next big event in Bible prophecy is the Second Coming of Jesus Christ. This includes the Pre-Tribulation Rapture of the Church prior to the Great Tribulation. This is because the Second Coming is pictured in the Scripture as a two-fold event mentioned in Hosea 6:3 (KJV) and James 5:7-8.

> James 5:7-8 says, "Be patient therefore, brethren, unto the coming of the Lord. Behold, the husbandman waiteth for the precious fruit of the earth, and hath long patience for it, until he receive the early and latter rain. Be ye also patient; stablish your hearts: for the coming of the Lord draweth nigh." (KJV)

The teaching of the Second Coming of Jesus Christ was of paramount importance to the New Testament believers. The promise of being saved from the terrible disasters to come during the Great Tribulation belongs to all believers who are in Christ whether they are Jews or Gentiles. There are promises of a Rapture that will happen before those terrible days.

> I Thessalonians 4:16-17 says, "For the Lord Himself will descend from heaven with a shout, with the voice of an archangel, and with the trumpet of God.

And the dead in Christ will rise first. Then we who are alive and remain shall be caught up together with them in the clouds to meet the Lord in the air. And thus we shall always be with the Lord." (NKJV)

Contrary to some who would say that the word "Rapture" wasn't brought up until the 19th Century, it is actually found in the Latin Vulgate translation by Saint Jerome who live around 400 AD. In that 17th verse he used these Latin words 'simul rapiemur cum illis in nubibus'. Translated to English it means 'caught up together with them in the clouds.'

Also, the Greek word in that passage used for "caught up" is 'harpazo.' This word means, "seize, catch away", or to "pluck up." It was taught and understood by Paul to mean to be taken up from this world and to be with Christ.

There are many scriptures that can be compiled for anyone to see and to believe in the Rapture of the Church. And there are many current events that are happening today that point the way to believing in the Rapture. The Word of God displays numerous reasons to believe in the Rapture of the Church. These reasons are seen in the Addendum.

Addendum
25 Reasons to Believe in the Rapture of the Church

1ˢᵗ Reason to believe in the Rapture of the Church.

The 7 year Great Tribulation period (week of seven – Daniel 9:27 KJV) was originally designed for the nation of Israel (not the Church) in the last days because of their rebellion against God (Deuteronomy 4:25-31 KJV) and because they rejected Christ (I Thessalonians 2:14-16 KJV). It will be a time of "Jacob's Trouble" (Jeremiah 30:7 KJV) like the nation of Israel has never seen before.

Michael, the chief prince for Israel (Daniel 12:1 KJV) stands with Israel to defend them as he fights against the Devil during this Great Tribulation (Revelation 12:7-14 KJV) in order for them to be saved (Romans 11:25-29 KJV). "Even so, Come, Lord Jesus".

Christ mentions to His Disciples that for the elect's sake, the Tribulation is shortened with its wrath apparently confined mostly to the second 3 ½ years (Matthew 24:21-22 KJV).

2ⁿᵈ Reason to believe in the Rapture of the Church.

Iniquity in full measure cannot start until the beginning of the Tribulation when God removes whatever it is that holds

the Antichrist back from being revealed (II Thessalonians 2:1-12 KJV). More than likely it is the life and power of the Church holding him back until it is removed.

In this passage, Paul tells the Thessalonians that the believers would be gathered together as in a Rapture before he mentions the day of Christ (day of the Lord, day of God) which is the day of destruction and vengeance at the end of the Great Tribulation.

He said in verse 1, "Now we beseech you, brethren, by the coming (pä-rü-sē'-ä – Greek word commonly used for Rapture) of our Lord Jesus Christ, and by our gathering together unto him." He encourages them by mentioning the Rapture first.

He then told them in verse 2, "That ye be not soon shaken in mind, or be troubled, neither by spirit, nor by word nor by letter as from us that the day of Christ (day of the Lord, day of God) is at hand (en-ē'-stā-mē – Greek word means "present, upon us"). That's the physical coming of the Lord bringing destruction and vengeance during and at the end of the Great Tribulation.

In other words, he describes our gathering unto Christ (Rapture) in verse 1 before the Day of Christ (Tribulation days) in verse 2. He was assuring them that they were not in the days of destruction and vengeance of the day of Christ and they did not miss the Rapture.

He states that the day of Christ (Tribulation days) was still in the future, saying, "Let no man deceive you by any means: for that day shall not come, except there come a falling away first, and that man of sin be revealed, the son of perdition" (verse 3). The first 3 ½ years of the Tribulation begins the wrath of God (Revelation chapters 6-11 KJV). The second 3 ½ years of the Tribulation is the worst of the wrath of God (Revelation chapters 12-19 KJV).

3rd Reason to believe in the Rapture of the Church.

True Believers (The Church) are promised deliverance from the wrath to come (Tribulation). (Luke 21:34-36 KJV; Romans 5:9 KJV; I Thessalonians 1:10; 5:9 KJV; II Peter 2:9 KJV)

The Great Tribulation of the visitation of the wrath of God is not for the believers. It shall come upon all those that do evil "who hold the truth in unrighteousness" (Romans 1:18 KJV); it shall come "upon the children of disobedience" (Ephesians 5:6 KJV; Colossians 3:5-6 KJV); and "upon all the world, to try them that dwell upon the earth" (Revelation 3:10 KJV).

4th Reason to believe in the Rapture of the Church.

A distinct promise is given to all true believers who have "kept the word of my patience" (hü-po-mo-nā' – Greek word is "Steadfast, endurance"), **so then God will keep them "from the hour of temptation"** (Revelation 3:10 KJV).

I believe this is the Rapture before the Tribulation. It was given to true believers of the church of Philadelphia (Greek word meaning "brotherly love") in the book of Revelation. This is a type of the true church of any era, and particularly in the last days who are living in the love of God.

5th Reason to believe in the Rapture of the Church.

Even though the word Rapture is not found in any English translation of the Bible, the Greek word 'här-pä'-zō' is.

This word is found in I Thessalonians 4:17 (KJV) and in the Greek it means "to seize, carry off by force, to snatch, or catch away."

Whether the early Church believed in the Rapture or were just dealing with some of the thinking of their day, early leaders spoke of it: <u>Irenaeus</u>, Cleric of Lyons in the 2nd Century wrote "the Church shall be suddenly caught up"; <u>Cyprian</u>, Bishop of Carthage in the 3rd Century mentions that Christians will have an "early departure" and be "delivered"; and <u>Ephraim</u>, a deacon in the 4th Century wrote "For all the saints and elect of God are gathered, prior to the tribulation that is to come, and are taken to the Lord."

Now it could be that they were only reporting about it in their writings. Nevertheless, it seems like John Darby did not invent the thought of a Rapture in the 19th Century as some have purported, because it appears like some people were believing it in the 2nd, 3rd, and 4th Centuries. Make no mistake, God does promise a Rapture for the Church.

6th Reason to believe in the Rapture of the Church.

The book of Revelation makes no mention of the Church ('ek-klā-sē'-ä'-called out ones) **being on earth** except in the first three chapters.

When John spoke about the Church while it was on earth in the first chapter, he said that Jesus "washed us from our sins in His own blood, and has <u>made us kings and priests unto God</u> and His Father" (Revelation 1:5-6 KJV).

Twenty four Elders are then seen by John in Heaven in the fifth chapter (Revelation 5:8-11 KJV) basically singing the same words that the Church did on earth in chapter one. They sang that He "<u>made us kings and priests to our God</u>; and we shall reign on the earth." Apparently those were Elders of the Church who were once on earth in chapter one but were now in Heaven around the Father's throne in chapter five. If the Elders were there, there is good reason to think that the Church would be there as well.

If the Elders of the Church are translated to Heaven as in a Rapture, then the Church has to be translated as well. They are raptured before the Tribulation starts because these Elders in Heaven see the scroll of the seal judgments in the hands of Jesus in chapter five as the first judgments to come upon the earth in the Tribulation. Jesus then opens them up in the next chapter of Revelation, chapter six, and that's when the Tribulation starts.

7th Reason to believe in the Rapture of the Church.

The 144,000 servants of God in Revelation 7:1-8 (KJV) are Jewish converts who speak about Jesus and the coming Kingdom in the Great Tribulation.

The Church does not preach this message because it preached it throughout the Church age. The Church is translated. That is why it mentions Jews as the servants of God who will speak this message to their nation and to the world. The message of the coming of the Lord and the coming of the Kingdom of Christ would now be in the hands of Jewish believers.

During this time of Tribulation, Israel will be converted through persecution when the Devil is cast to the earth after warfare with Michael (Revelation 12:7-12 KJV) who is the archangel that stands to protect the Jews (Daniel 12:1-2 KJV). This is why the 144,000 are formed to preach their message so that innumerable multitudes will be saved. This multitude is pictured in Heaven at the end of the Tribulation (Revelation 7:9-17 KJV).

If the church was in the Tribulation, what will they be doing? If it was in the Tribulation, God would more than likely use the true

Church to preach this message. But it is not preaching. That is why the Tribulation is not about the Church. It is about the nation of Israel who will be converted in the future (Romans 11:25-29 KJV). Israel as a nation has never believed the Church concerning Jesus so they need to hear it from their fellow Jews during this Tribulation time.

The conversion of the Jews and their entrance into the 1,000 year Millennium on earth helps Christ and the Church rule on the earth. In part it is in fulfillment of the Covenant that God made with Abraham as an everlasting covenant (Genesis 17:7-8 KJV).

8th Reason to believe in the Rapture of the Church.

One of the two witnesses in Revelation 11:3-14 (KJV) is usually depicted as Elijah that comes back to earth during the Tribulation (Malachi 4:4-6 KJV) **with great power and authority.**

The other witness at that time is usually believed to be Moses or Enoch. Elijah and this other witness are the two who stand by the Lord of the whole earth (Zechariah 4:11-14 KJV). Their ministries have control over nature, and they fight against the enemies of God.

If the church was in the Tribulation, perhaps Peter, James or John would return to earth and God would use them. But the Church is gone and the Jews have never believed the New Testament disciples anyway, so they need hear it from two of their great Old Testament Patriarchs during the Tribulation.

9th Reason to believe in the Rapture of the Church.

In Revelation 12 during the Tribulation, Satan persecutes a woman, who in that chapter is usually designated as the nation of Israel.

We know that the church is already raptured, otherwise the church being the very body of Christ is just as likely to be persecuted as the nation of Israel. The reason Israel is persecuted is because God must honor, fulfill, and complete His covenant promise He made with that nation (Genesis 17:7-21 KJV; Psalm 105:8-11 KJV; Jeremiah 31:31-37 KJV) and restore them in preparation for the coming Millennium.

10th Reason to believe in the Rapture of the Church.

In Heaven the overcomers who gained the victory over the Antichrist, are seen singing the song of Moses the servant of God, and the song of the Lamb after the Tribulation is over (Revelation 15:2-3 KJV).

This is not the Church. It is the Tribulation saints who have gone through the Tribulation who sing the song of Moses (Exodus 15:1-21 KJV; Deuteronomy 32:1-47 KJV; Psalm 90:1-17 KJV) and the Lamb.

The Church does not sing the song of Moses nor has it ever sung the song of Moses because they were not established through the Jewish faith. They were established through Jesus Christ. The Church teaches about Moses, but the Church that knows Jesus Christ can only sing the song of the Lamb (Revelation 5:6-14 KJV). Its salvation is in response to its belief in Jesus Christ during the Church period.

Therefore, those who sing the song of Moses and the Lamb are Jewish believers and other converts (Gentiles), who during the Tribulation period had lived the Jewish Traditions that pointed to a belief in Jesus Christ. They also preached about the coming Kingdom because of the witness of the 144,000 Jewish believers. Again, only Tribulation saints can sing this because of the preaching of the Jewish faith, and their association with Jesus during the Tribulation.

11th Reason to believe in the Rapture of the Church.

The Lord coming as a "thief in the night" is not for a waiting and prepared Church at the beginning of the Tribulation. True believers are looking forward to the Coming of the Lord and should not be unprepared as if Christ would come as a thief. The Lord comes as a "thief" for an unsuspecting evil world and for a backsliding Church. The "thief" scriptures given in the Bible point to events at the end of the Great Tribulation and not at the beginning of the Tribulation when the Rapture occurs. The scriptures are I Thessalonians 5:1-4 (KJV); II Peter 3:8-10 (KJV); Revelation 3:3 KJV (type of the unprepared Church); Revelation 16:15-16 (KJV); Matthew 24:42-43 (KJV). The Greek word there in Matthew 24:42-43 (KJV) is e'r-kho-mī and it means to 'arrive or return' which of course refers to Christ's coming as a thief at the end of the Tribulation.

12th Reason to believe in the Rapture of the Church.

Scriptures urge an attitude of constant expectation of Christ's coming - Acts 1:11 (KJV); I Corinthians 15:51-52 (KJV); I Thessalonians 1:10 (KJV); I Timothy 6:14 (KJV); Hebrews 9:28 (KJV); James 5:8 (KJV). If the church goes through the Tribulation, then believers would be looking for Tribulation signs and events rather than Christ's return in the Rapture. Paul's epistles which are given primarily for the instruction of the church contain no warning to the church that it must go through the Tribulation.

13th Reason to believe in the Rapture of the Church.

There is precedence in scripture that shows how God protected His people before judgment fell on the earth.

a. Enoch escaped death and the evil of the pre-flood world - Genesis 5:24 (KJV);Hebrews 11:5 (KJV).

b. Noah and his family were saved from the flood — Genesis 7:1 (KJV); II Peter 2:5 (KJV).

c. Lot was delivered from Sodom and Gomorrah – Genesis 19:29 (KJV); II Peter 2:7 (KJV).

d. Jesus, Mary and Joseph fled to Egypt before Herod murders children –Matthew 2:13-15 (KJV).

I believe the same thing can and will happen to the Church.

14th Reason to believe in the Rapture of the Church.

The Church is a heavenly people with a heavenly calling and destiny, and will be called out of this wicked world – Hebrews 3:1, 6 (KJV); Ephesians 1:11-14 (KJV). Israel that will be brought back to God through tribulation is an earthly people, with a promise of earthly destiny and inheritance – Deuteronomy 28:1-14 (KJV).

The promise of the heavenly calling of the Church is clearly seen in scripture.

a) The church was chosen before the foundation of the world - Ephesians 1:3-4 (KJV).

b) The church is not of the world - John 17:14-16 (KJV); Philippians 3:20 (KJV).

c) The church is raised with Christ to sit in the Heavenly realm -Ephesians 1:3; 2:4-7 (KJV).

d) The church is foreordained to be conformed to the image of Christ - Romans 8:28-29 (KJV).

e) The church was promised a heavenly position - John 14:1-3 (KJV); Hebrews 12:22-24 (KJV)

15ᵗʰ Reason to believe in the Rapture of the Church.

In Matthew 24:27-31 (KJV), two different Greek words are used for the 'coming' of Christ.

In verse 27 at the first mention of His 'coming', the Greek word pä-rü-sē'-ä ("presence, to be near, alongside") is used. It is a picture of the Rapture at the beginning of the Great Tribulation. Verse 28 then says that this event will happen just as sure as wherever there is a dead body, "there will the eagles be gathered together."

The Tribulation is mentioned as happening in verse 29.

In verse 30 at the second mention of His 'coming', a different Greek word e'r-kho-mī ("to arrive") is used. This is the literal Second Coming of Christ.

A progression of these events in the End-Times are pictured here as (1) Coming, "to be near" as in the Rapture (2) Tribulation, and (3) Coming, "literally come" as in the Second Coming.

The two different Greek words indicate a two-fold coming, at the beginning and at the end of the Tribulation. In verse 27, Christ's Coming is depicted as lightning flashing across the sky and not touching the ground. It indicates Christ's presence that appears in the sky and the Church is caught up to meet Him at that time before the Tribulation starts in verse 29. This Coming of Christ for the

Church happens as well as, or "alongside" of Christ's literal Second Coming in verses 30-31 after the Tribulation.

Today, we derive many of our words in the English language using that "alongside" idea from that first syllable 'pä-rü,' that is used in the Greek word pä-rü-sē'-ä. It means something that is two-fold or something else that is alongside, aids in, or helps to define the word.

Examples in the English language that are from that first syllable 'pä-rü are as follows:

1) **Parable** – allegorical story whose meaning is behind some religious principle or moral lesson.
2) **Paraclete** – the Greek word for the Holy Spirit, sent by Christ, who is an aid to the Christian.
3) **Paradise** – an intermediate place where the righteous depart to, awaiting the final heaven.
4) **Paragraph** – two or more sentences in a statement.
5) **Parallel** – two items that are alongside each other.
6) **Paramedic** – one who assists in the work of a physician.
7) **Paraphrase** – the restatement of the text.

Hence, the Rapture of the Church at the beginning of the Great Tribulation happens 'alongside' of the Second Coming of Christ at the end of the Great Tribulation.

16th Reason to believe in the Rapture of the Church.

The Lord does not set foot on the earth when coming for the church in the Rapture at the beginning of the Tribulation, but meets the saints in the air - I Thessalonians 4:16-17 (KJV). His coming for Israel's salvation at the end of the Tribulation is when he literally comes to the earth ("...His feet shall stand ... upon the Mount of Olives..." - Zechariah 14:3-4 (KJV). That is when He returns to earth with the Bride of Christ, the Church (Revelation 19:7-9, 11, and 14 KJV). He will then set up His Kingdom for 1,000 years on the earth, which is the Millennium.

17th Reason why I believe in the Rapture of the Church.

The Lord's coming is a two-fold blessing, like the former and latter rain in Israel during harvest. The "Former rain" refers to rains that came in the fall. The "Latter rain" refers to rains that came in the spring.

Scripture tells us that the former and latter rains can be compared to the Second Coming of Christ, (James 5:7-8 KJV; Hosea 6:3 KJV). James 5:7-8 (KJV) says, "Be patient therefore, brethren, unto the coming of the Lord. Behold, the husbandman waits for the precious fruit of the earth, and hath long patience for it, until he receive the early and latter rain. Be ye also patient; stablish your hearts: for the coming of the Lord draws nigh."

The indication of a two-fold plan as the former and latter rain can show both a Rapture and a literal Second Coming. The former rain would be God's plan to catch away the Church at the beginning of the tribulation. The latter rain would be the Second Coming at the end of the Tribulation to restore the Covenant relationship that God has with His chosen people Israel.

That Second Coming latter rain would also include the fall of wrath upon the world in the Great Tribulation because of their sin and because of their treatment of Israel (Joel 3:1-2).

18th Reason to believe in the Rapture of the Church.

The Church, wearing white garments as the Bride of Christ at the Marriage Supper of the Lamb in Heaven, is seen dressed in

those same white garments when Christ returns to the earth at the end of the Tribulation (Revelation 19:7-9, 11, 14 (KJV). This indicates an earlier Rapture. Christ cannot return with His saints from Heaven at the end of the Tribulation (Jude 14 KJV; Revelation 19:7-14 KJV) unless they were already taken up into Heaven in the first place and are with Him when He returns.

19ᵗʰ Reason to believe in the Rapture of the Church.

The kingdom of Antichrist is characterized by gross darkness (Revelation 16:10-11 KJV) **with no faith.** This is not true of the faithful church – (Ephesians 5:8 KJV; Colossians 1:12-13 KJV); (I Thessalonians 5:4-5 KJV; I Peter 2:9 KJV). The church, which is built on faith (Galatians 2:16, 20 KJV) with believers who are the light of the world (Matthew 5:14-16 KJV), is the total antithesis of the darkness of the Antichrist kingdom. The evil darkness of the world has never believed the light that is within the church. The church is removed from earth so that God can deal with the darkness for all eternity.

20ᵗʰ Reason to believe in the Rapture of the Church.

Five separate crowns are promised to the believing Church in the New Testament. James 1:12 KJV (Crown of Life); I Corinthians 9:25 KJV (Crown Incorruptible); I Thessalonians 2:19 KJV (Crown of Rejoicing); II Timothy 4:8 KJV (Crown of Righteousness); I Peter 5:1-4 KJV (Crown of Glory). These crowns are meant for the believing Church who receive their rewards before the Tribulation begins. There are no crowns mentioned for those who become believers in the book of Revelation during the Tribulation, indicating a difference in rewards for the two groups.

21ˢᵗ Reason to believe in the Rapture of the Church.

God has a plan for the Covenant Jewish nation and the rest of the world and it is clear in the Book of Romans. God offers them Salvation, brings them through Tribulation, and then establishes them in the Millennium.

   (a) SALVATION comes to every believer: to the Jew first and also to the Greek Romans 1:16 KJV.

   (b) TRIBULATION and ANGUISH comes to those who do evil: of the Jew first and also of the Gentile - Romans 2:9 KJV.

   (c) GLORY, HONOR and PEACE (Millennium) comes to those who do well: to the Jew first, and also to the Gentile - Romans 2:10 KJV.

22ⁿᵈ Reason to believe in the Rapture of the Church.

The Scriptures dealing with the Tribulation have particular reference to the Jews and not the Church - Matthew 24:1-35 KJV; Mark 13:1-31 KJV; Luke 21:5-33 KJV.

   a. The setting is in Judea.

   b. They were to pray that their flight would not be on the Sabbath (a Jewish concern).

   c. The abomination spoken of by Daniel is to be set up in Jerusalem.

   d. The "tribes" (Greek = fü-lä' - Israel, or any nation) mourn - Zechariah 12:8-11 KJV; Matthew 24:30 KJV, not the church.

   e. The appearance of the "elect" in those sections of these three chapters refer to the Jews and not the church.

23rd Reason to believe in the Rapture of the Church.

Some biblical translations seem to depict two separate groups in Heaven at the end of the Tribulation when the Millennium begins (Revelation 20:4 KJV). The first group are those who are already sitting on thrones in Heaven who would have been given judgment powers. I believe this to be the Raptured Church because the Church has been given this kind of promise and authority (Revelation 3:21 KJV; I Corinthians 6:2-3 KJV). The second group are those who had just gone through the Tribulation and had overcome the Antichrist and had given their lives for the cause of Christ during the Tribulation. They too lived and reigned with Christ.

24th Reason to believe in the Rapture of the Church.

The Lord illustrated to his disciples (representing Israel) **to wait like those who are waiting for their master as He returns from a wedding banquet** (Luke 12:35-38 KJV). This is a picture of Christ the Lamb after He is married to the Church (Revelation 19:7-9 KJV) and then returns with the Church at the end of the Tribulation (Revelation 19:14 KJV) to reign with the nation of Israel during the Millennium (Revelation 20:4 KJV).

25th Reason to believe in the Rapture of the Church.

It seems reasonable that an interval of time between the coming of Christ for His saints (I Thessalonians 4:15-18 KJV)**, and then coming with them** (Revelation 19:11-14 KJV)**, would be required for the rewards of believers** (I Corinthians 3:12-15 KJV), **and their marriage to Christ** (Revelation 19:7-9 KJV). This happens in Heaven during the Tribulation after the Church's Rapture. Marriage to Christ can be compared to a Hebrew marriage that has three stages:

(a) -The legal marriage (Salvation. We are bought with a price – (I Corinthians 6:20 KJV).
(b) -The groom takes his bride from her parent's home (Rapture. We are caught up together – (I Thessalonians 4:16-17 KJV).
(c) -The wedding supper or feast (Marriage of the Lamb. The Wife has been made ready – (Revelation 19:-8 KJV)

About the Author

David Siriano is a graduate of Zion (Northpoint) Bible College in Haverhill, MA and has his degree in Bible. He served as a Pastor in the New England States and New York for 45 years until 2008. No longer Pastoring, he is now available to travel and conduct End Times Bible prophecy seminars nationwide.

Throughout his ministry, he has had an avid interest in Eschatology, the study of End Time events. He has devoted much of his 57 years of ministry, studying and teaching on that subject. As a social eschatologist, he has conducted numerous seminars in the states of New York, Massachusetts, Connecticut, Rhode Island, Maine, Vermont, New Hampshire, Pennsylvania, Maryland, Florida and throughout the east coast on the End-Times message of the Bible and how it relates to the news events of today.

He specializes in the Biblical Apocalyptic books of Daniel and Revelation, the Old Testament Tabernacle, and the Major and Minor Prophets. He has taught at the New York District School of Ministry, as college guest lecturer and teacher at Northpoint Bible College in Haverhill, MA, and at Crossroads Cathedral International Bible Institute in East Hartford, CT.

His other Books are:

The Cultural Collapse of America, and the World
Intergalactic Warfare
A Look Beyond

Lightning Source UK Ltd.
Milton Keynes UK
UKHW021844190520
363382UK00006B/378